Jess humbly shares her wisdom and relatable experiences, challenging us on the intersection of grace and holiness. By asking us tough questions, we are surprisingly jolted into action and given ammo to fervently run on mission.

JENA HOLLIDAY, inspirational artist, SpoonfulOfFaith .com

When you pick up this book expect to be challenged, moved, and always pointed back to the Lord. *Dance, Stand, Run* isn't about striving, but about being changed by God. Jess is masterful at discerning the challenges of our generation and speaking truth right to it.

HAYLEY MORGAN, coauthor of *Wild and Free* and social entrepreneur

At the center of the Father's heart for you and I is the grace He's lavished onto us, the holy invitation for us to become more like Jesus, and His purposeful mission for each one of us. After reading *Dance, Stand, Run*, you will see Jess's heart burns for us to wake up and walk in the abundance God has extended to you and me through grace, holiness, and mission.

NICK CONNOLLY, husband to Jess and pastor of GospelCommunity.com

ALSO BY JESS CONNOLLY

Wild and Free with Hayley Morgan

PRAISE FOR

DANCE, STAND, RUN

Jess is a friend who challenges me to the core. Her candor and conviction in *Dance, Stand, Run* left a mark on my heart. Take your time, let the words settle deep. You'll be changed and grateful.

REBEKAH LYONS, author of *You Are Free* and *Freefall to Fly*

Dance, Stand, Run is like water to my thirsty, overwhelmed, fast-paced heart. In words as sweet and conversational as those coming from a dear friend across a coffee shop table, Jess reminds us that we are made for so much, but that so little is required to soak in God's grace. *Dance, Stand, Run* has truly inspired me to my core to reevaluate the why in my life and to embrace the woman God has called me to be in an even bigger way.

EMILY LEY, author of *Grace, Not Perfection* and
A Simplified Life

Jess is a voice our generation needs in its ears. She loves God with everything in her and shows us all throughout this book what it means to desire holiness in our lives. She goes first, telling us her struggles and triumphs, and then invites us to journey this path as well. Get your pen ready, because you'll be underlining this whole book!

JAMIE IVEY, podcaster, *The Happy Hour with Jamie Ivey*

Dance, Stand, Run, is far more than a great read—it's a life-altering experience! These pages shook me to my core and made me cheer out loud as Jess uncovered life-giving truth after truth. Most of all, *Dance, Stand, Run* gave me a new and fiery passion to do just that: dance in His grace, stand on holy ground, and run with God on mission. When the truth of God's Word gets ahold of you, it changes the very molecules of your heart. Jess hands over the truth of transforming grace and holiness with humility and courage. Dear friends, I don't casually invite you to read this book; I urge you to! There is no greater joy than knowing the heartbeat of our Father—no greater freedom or fuel. *Dance, Stand, Run* leads us to His feet and illuminates the most beautiful life path one can enjoy: His. Dance to the bookstore, stand firm to reach for a dozen copies for you and friends, and run home to read this book, knowing you're about to be changed!

LARA CASEY, author of *Make It Happen* and *Cultivate*

Some are dreamers, some are doers, but Jess is a dreamer who does. This is a go-getter's guide to moving, dancing, and running while doing it all with grace—the soulful kind of grace that Jess herself has discovered because she has lived it.

JESSICA HONEGGER, founder and CEO of Noonday Collection

If there is anyone who so fervently strives for the balance between grace and holiness, it's Jess. In her presence, I have been offered both pause and power, both hush and hustle. In her signature disarming honesty, Jess manages to spur us on and settle us down, all in one dripping-with-love invitation.

ERIN LOECHNER, founder of DesignforMankind.com and author of *Chasing Slow*

DANCE

THE GOD-INSPIRED MOVES

STAND

OF A WOMAN ON

RUN

HOLY GROUND

Jess Connolly

ZONDERVAN

Dance, Stand, Run
Copyright © 2017 by Jessica Ashleigh Connolly

Requests for information should be addressed to:
Zondervan, 3900 Sparks Dr. SE, Grand Rapids, Michigan 49546

ISBN 978-0-310-34984-6 (audio)

ISBN 978-0-310-34565-7 (ebook)

Library of Congress Cataloging-in-Publication Data

Names: Connolly, Jess, author.
Title: Dance, stand, run : the God-inspired moves of a woman on holy ground / Jess Connolly.
Description: Grand Rapids, Michigan : Zondervan, [2017]
Identifiers: LCCN 2017026913 | ISBN 9780310345640 (softcover)
Subjects: LCSH: Christian women--Religious life. | Holiness.
Classification: LCC BV4527 .C64395 2017 | DDC 248.8/43--dc23 LC record available at
      https://lccn.loc.gov/2017026913

Published in association with literary agent Jenni Burke of D.C. Jacobson & Associates LLC, an Author Management Company, www.dcjacobson.com

Cover image: Creative Market
Interior design: Kait Lamphere

First printing August 2017 / Printed in the United States of America

CONTENTS

OUR *DANCE, STAND, RUN* DECLARATION

We are the daughters of God. We delight and dance in God's grace, and we don't want to take it for granted. We've been found out, found needing Him, and we won't go back into hiding again.

We are the daughters of God, and we stand firm on holy ground. We didn't get here by merit. We were bought and brought by the blood of Jesus. Here we stand, and here we'll stay. Our positioning and proximity to God means something, and both invite direction over our daily lives and decisions. We are here on purpose, a part of the world, set apart to be used by God to bring change. We don't conform to our environment or seek its approval. We grow spiritually while our bodies groan, and we live in this now-and-not-yet reality as saints in a fallen world.

We are the daughters of God; we are compelled by His grace and held by His holiness imputed to us through Jesus. We don't soak up the abundance of intimacy with God mindlessly, but we grab hold of all He has to offer us so we can give it away to everyone else. We run on mission, because when you hold the keys to light and life, you don't hide them.

We are the daughters of God, and we are ready to dance, stand, and run in faith for His glory and our good.

A NOTE FROM JESS

This isn't the kind of book you write alone or read alone. The theological weight of this writing was important to me, and I didn't want to get that wrong, but there was something else that pushed me to pull in my friends on this project. I wanted to make sure that the people I do life with, the people who know me well, could vouch for my words and stand beside me as I recorded them. When you're writing bold things about holiness, grace, and mission, you want to be sure that people who are part of your actual life will co-sign on what you have to say.

I wanted my friends to ensure that these words were gracious and genuine. I wanted them to check that the stories weren't self-indulgent or misleading. And most of all, I needed their covering of prayer—over my heart and yours.

This book wasn't written alone. In fact, at the beginning of each chapter, you'll see the name of a woman from my life. I asked these women to give honest feedback, to shift the content or to shift me on my position regarding the content. I'm so grateful for them, and I know you would be too if you saw the passion and prayer they put into this job.

This book wasn't meant to be read alone, so I strongly encourage you to read it with a friend (or a bunch of friends) and answer the questions at the end of each chapter together. Don't hold back when you answer—dance in grace, stand in holiness, and run forward together by being genuine in your community as you sort through these words. This book is for you, and the fruit ahead, I pray, is all for Him. I love you women so much. Let's go.

Jess

PROLOGUE:
PRETTY LITTLE LIARS

THE BOOK I DIDN'T SET OUT TO WRITE

Read by Kelly Cowan*

We sat beside each other in the back of the church, with our knees touching and our deflated hearts mirroring the same overwhelming discouragement. Everyone else sat in front of us, their backs to us as they sang the last few worship songs, oblivious to the spiral of defeat we were swirling in a few feet behind them. My husband and I couldn't be much further from the typical pastor and pastor's wife, or so we're told. He loves to cook and is much better at laundry than I am. We argue over who is the bigger introvert. I don't play the piano or help with children's ministry, no one has ever in my whole life described me as sweet or quiet, and in the past year I've had pink hair a handful of times. Whether or not we fit the stereotypical description of a family in

---

* See A Note from Jess for more on this.

church ministry, at that moment I imagine we felt what thousands of ministers of the gospel had felt before us, and I imagine we'll feel it again in the future.

It was Easter 2016, our third Easter together as a church, and we'd anticipated it. Holy anticipation, sacred expectation—we were both hoping for some revival. We'd made invitation cards for everyone in our church weeks before and asked them to pray over who they wanted to invite. We'd held prayer gatherings to ask for God's power to be displayed among our people that day. Nick, my husband, had prepped an amazing sermon and then preached his heart out.

But friends? It just didn't go down like we had pictured. Nick had seen a few people fall asleep during the sermon, and from where we sat in the back, we could see people looking bored, using their phones during worship. I am sure God moved in people's hearts and shifted things in the spiritual space, but outwardly it looked like any other Sunday, or even a little worse. It felt like the dreaded "off Sunday," which flew in the face of the Sunday we'd anticipated, planned, prayed over, and hoped for.

So we sat in the back like two young kids who'd lost their little league game. We tried to encourage each other a little bit, rallied enough to say good-bye to everyone, tore down our mobile church (we meet in an elementary school), and took our kids to lunch to celebrate Easter. We didn't talk much for the rest of the day about what had happened that morning but instead shifted gears and discussed what the upcoming spring break would look like for our family.

The tension was thick. We'd hoped God was going to show up and do something incredible. We'd hoped for life change at least and revival at best. We were doing all of this for God, so wasn't He going to show us His presence and His power?

The next morning, in a quiet moment, I let myself pull the string a little bit. As I spent time with the Lord, I got honest and open with my Father and told Him how I felt about our Easter. I cried about my unmet expectations and what seemed like the lackluster spiritual state of our church. I told Him how hard it was to be a church planter's wife, and it was feeling particularly difficult with so little visible fruit and outward change. And then finally, when I was done telling Him how I felt about it, I decided to be quiet for a moment and let Him tell me how *He* felt. I asked if there was any correction or reproof for me, any part of this problem in which I'd been complicit without realizing it.

It's worth noting that I sure didn't anticipate a rebuke. I thought He might give me some piece of Scripture or sense that we were doing all we could do and confirm that this was simply everyone else's fault. True story.

I didn't sit long before something interesting happened in my brain. As I replayed the day, three particular conversations stood out. If my memory of the day was like a fluid stream of water before, now there were three ugly boulders disrupting the stream—three big boulders that didn't belong there. And these recollections didn't have anything to do with other people's sins or issues—they were about me. I had had three separate conversations with three separate women in our church that Easter morning, all of them eerily similar and kind of embarrassing to remember. And if they were embarrassing in my own mind, you can only imagine how humbling it is for me to share them with you now. But that's where we gotta start, sisters. Someone has to go first.

I'd gone to each of these women individually and told them about something that was on my mind, something I felt compelled to share and excited to talk about. I'd initiated these conversations—with my friends, these women of God, on this super-spiritual and holy day of Easter—with an agenda. I point this out in such an explicit way because you need to picture it fully: these conversations didn't happen accidentally, and no one was trying to fill the space or make light banter. I went there *with intention*.

What I had to share wasn't a new passage of Scripture that was impacting me or a truth God was revealing in my heart. It wasn't a burden I was praying through or an answer to prayer I was eager to communicate.

What did I go out of my way to talk about to those three daughters of God that fine Easter Sunday? The show *Pretty Little Liars*. (Don't shut the book. I promise this is going somewhere.)

Now let me back up, in case you're not familiar with *Pretty Little Liars*, or *PLL* for short. Wikipedia describes it as "an American teen drama, mystery-thriller television series based loosely on the popular book series of the same title." Wikipedia also tells us it was meant to be "*Desperate Housewives* for teens," a theory I can corroborate. One magazine called it a cross between *I Know What You Did Last Summer* and *Gossip Girl*. So, yeah—that's the gist.

I just felt this utter compulsion to talk to the women in my church about it on that fine Easter Sunday because I'd begun watching it and couldn't get enough. Did I talk about how expectant we were for worship that day? No. Did I share with them how Nick and I had been fasting and praying for our people to experience the Lord on Easter Sunday? No. Did I ask them how God was moving in their hearts and lives? Give them an opportunity to testify to His great love and mercy? No. I just told them about this semi-raunchy, teenage murder-mystery TV show I'd been watching. *And then I plopped myself down in the back of the church wondering why we weren't in the midst of revival.*

And so I sat there the following morning, feeling all the love and grace and mercy from my Father, who knows I make mistakes over and over again. I didn't feel condemnation or shame, but a warm conviction spread through me. My heart began to beat faster, and my head throbbed with one very loud question: *Have I forgotten about holiness?*

What shift in my spirit had caused me to talk about something so profane when, in reality, I was so spiritually expectant? How often was I doing this—living on the outside like someone who isn't thinking about God all the time, when on the inside my heart is solely for Him? Was this how I was leading others? Ignoring the sacred to fit in and seem normal?

Had I grabbed grace and abandoned the call to be set apart? Had I missed the abundance available to me by walking the mysterious duality of relationship with God—grace *and* truth? I talk a lot and think a lot about freedom, about what I've been freed from. But suddenly I was wondering: Why don't I think about where I've been freed *to*? If I was taken out of darkness, condemnation, and the shackles of sin, then where does my soul currently reside?

I wondered: *Am I on holy ground? If so, how is that compelling me to live, and why, for the love, am I talking about* Pretty Little Liars *on Easter Sunday? Have I forgotten about holiness?*

I sat in my bed, having the most honest moment with the Lord, holding my coffee cup and looking out the window with clarity, confirming this one thing in my soul: *Yes, I think I forgot about holiness.*

Then I got out of bed and marched into my husband's home office, where I began talking and confessing and conjecturing in circles and loops. I went through the whole story and laid my questions bare for him, telling him I had this rooted sense in my soul that maybe I wasn't the only one, maybe a lot of us had forgotten about holiness. He nodded and affirmed my verbal ramblings with a slight smile as he continued to let me process.

Then I started asking friends in whispers at coffee shops, "Do you think we've forgotten about holiness? Do you think it's just me? Is this a thing?" Their blank stares were followed by slow nods, maybe an errant tear or two running down their cheeks. After I confessed, they confessed in return. Though none of us had talked about it, we'd all felt some version of an ache in the back of our hearts. We were all living with some awareness of the tension between what we believe about God and what our lives *say* we believe about God. None of us wanted to tumble into legalism or spiritual perfectionism, but we were all feeling something here, a conviction that maybe something was amiss.

I couldn't help but think back on times where a friend confessed some sin to me and I plastered "grace" all over her with my words, dismissing her conviction. Memories of times I asked for grace in the wake of hurting someone, skipping casually over the process of repentance and restoration, suddenly stood out to me vividly. There were so many times I'd invoked grace for myself and others, and in these instances it seemed we traded what could have been sharpening and growth for easy dismissal.

We give ourselves grace about nitpicking at our husbands, not spending time with the Lord, misusing our finances, telling little white lies, having bad attitudes, and losing it on those around us in the midst of stressful days. We give ourselves grace, but somewhere along the way we stopped letting that grace transform us as it is meant to. And I wondered: *Has this caused us to lose sight of our holy standing with God?*

As I shared these ideas with my people, we realized that we talk about grace, mission, mothering, and our dreams. We talk about fashion, culture, the books we're reading, leaders we love, and things we're praying about. But we don't talk about holiness—ours or God's.

Oftentimes on Friday mornings, the women in our community meet for sunrise prayer at the beach. Sometimes there are twenty of us, sometimes there are three of us, and oftentimes it's just me. The Friday after Easter I met a few gals for our usual prayer time, and with shaky hands I told them, "I feel a tug to pull this string and linger on this question, asking it first for myself, and then for our generation: Have we forgotten about holiness, and have we traded our pursuit of the things above for a grace that is not compelling us to much at all?" They were honest and told me the question stung, but that they were glad I had asked it. Laughing, they shook their heads, gently joking with me about how I ought to write a book on the topic, about what a hard book that would be to write and maybe not an easy one to read, but I should think on it.

Here's where I should tell you that this is not the book I set out to write. But it has become the book I most need, and friend, I hope the same will be true for you.

My next step was to write a frightened email to my editor and agent, asking if I could change what was intended to be a lighthearted book into a pretty deep one. Jenni is my agent, and Stephanie is my editor, and they're busy women, and I respect them more than I could ever say. I didn't expect to hear back from them for weeks, but their emails appeared in my inbox much sooner than I anticipated, and they were saying the same thing everyone else was: *It won't be easy, but you should do it. Let's change the book: let's write about holiness.*

Finally I made my older sister, who was in Africa at the time, drop what she was doing and read a few paragraphs I'd written. Did she think I was crazy? Did she think I was abandoning grace or falling off the liberty wagon? Did she, too, resonate with this— this righteous, rumbling fear that maybe we've forgotten about holiness? These are the kinds of things you need your big sister to sign off on, even when she's five thousand miles away. We talked on FaceTime as she walked around, pacing the dirt floor of the missions base. She blinked back some tears, blessed the idea, and sent me on my way to write.

One by one, the people I love looked at me with kind eyes and quiet affirmations. They felt it in their hearts too, and they saw it in their communities. They felt the pangs of conviction deep in their ribs during conversations with other believers, and they experienced the dull ache of confusion when a group of professed Jesus followers seem to slink away in apathy from spiritual things, moving instead toward the things of this world. My people confessed that they, too, had wondered if our doctrine of grace had somehow eclipsed our understanding of holiness, rather than the two working together to help us live in awe of the Lord. And each of them said, "Yes, if you can write this with humility and a large dose of hope, this is the book you should write."

THE WRONG GIRL

If I'm honest, friends, this is the part where I want to slam my laptop closed and pick a new book topic. Because this is perilous and dangerous ground we're about to wade through. The first few days I felt the tug to write *this* book (instead of the one I had planned to write), I told my Father in prayer, *"You've got the wrong girl!* I'm the wild and free girl. I'm the gospel girl! I love grace, and I am messy, and I have never stayed inside the lines. Ever. I cannot be the one to talk about holiness." I told Him I'd rather be responsible for writing about things that make people feel good, excited, and ready to tackle the world.

But in His gentleness, the Lord bolstered my heart. I felt free to stand in the truth that it's the wild and free women, the ones who love the gospel and soak up grace, who *need* to talk about holiness. I started to believe that strong words can carry the most hope, and when we allow ourselves to feel conviction, we are comforted by the Holy Spirit.

I'm not sure if you're like me, if you've avoided talking about holiness because you've discounted yourself. Maybe there have been conversations you've wanted to steer toward a more righteous tone, but you've thought surely you'd be misunderstood or discouraged from taking it too far. I wonder if there are moments you've wanted to push, prod, or ask a hard question, but you've been certain the people you're talking to will only see your past sin and your faults. In those moments, isn't it easier to stick to the safe waters of grace, rather than stir things up with talk of holiness or higher callings? When our reputation is at stake, isn't it often easier to take the more cautious path that doesn't expose us to the accountability our own hearts are craving?

Maybe you've had these hunger pains for holiness but you haven't wanted to make anyone else feel uncomfortable. You could be surrounded by believers who are seemingly older and wiser, and you're waiting for them to start the conversation. I'm willing to bet that a large number of you have tried and have been shut down. I'll never forget the story of my good friend, who felt a stirring in her spirit to read more of God's Word with the women in her church. She shared this desire with her pastor, asking if she could start a Bible study, and was told that it might shame other women who don't like to read the Bible but instead prefer Christian books. Some of us only have to push through the perception and fear that our holy desires are too much; others of us have had those fears confirmed.

Or maybe, on the other side of the fence, you've fallen so in love with the grace message that's been leading the charge in recent church history that you've felt nothing but *relief*. It's certain that the American church is experiencing a surge of freedom, and it's a beautiful thing. I've heard it called various things: the Grace Movement, the New Grace Reformation, the Hyper-Grace Movement. Whatever it's called, the message is clear: For the past few decades, the American church has been receiving and believing the idea that we've been set free from our sin and made clean in a whole new light, with a whole new fervor.

We're listening to contemporary worship music, maybe even singing secular songs depending on where you attend church. People can now wear jeans to church in almost every city across the country, whereas that was an anomaly thirty years ago. We've got bumper stickers declaring that it's about relationship, not religion— it's grace, not rules—New Testament, not Old Testament!

I've sat with women in churches across America and heard them say things like, "It wasn't until five years ago that I started to *get grace*," or "You know, at the church I grew up in, we didn't talk much about grace. We talked a lot about what we needed to do, but a lot of what I'm hearing now is new and fresh." In some regions, they've been talking about grace longer or in different lights, but most people watching the church culture spectrum will agree—we weren't embracing grace, the way we are now, fifty or sixty years ago.

It wasn't that I was *trying* to forget about holiness, it's just that I heard about grace so much more. And I needed it! I *needed* to hear the good news of grace. I needed the balm that settled me and spoke at-ease-ness over my soul. I needed the good news that Jesus is enough and His forgiveness is all-encompassing to assuage the intrinsic feeling that I'm not enough. So maybe you're like me, and it wasn't that you wanted to walk away from holiness, but that you let it slip past you in celebration of grace.

I also recognize there are a slew of women out there who are nothing like me, and maybe by this point in the chapter you're feeling frustrated and riled up, thinking, *I didn't forget about holiness! Don't speak for me!* Maybe you've thought a ton about righteousness, about being set apart, God's holiness, our standing with Him, and the truth that how we live and act and move is a reflection of what we believe about who He is. But I wonder if you're like those of my friends on the end of the spectrum who've said they remembered holiness all along but have felt the ache in their bones from a lack of ability to trust in true, abundant grace.

There are telltale signs and symptoms when we swing too far one way or the other. I find that when we swing toward holiness and away from grace, we spend much of our days measuring— measuring how far and how good we are against the world around us, measuring the sin and fallen-ness of everyone else and fearing it might seep into our tidy, protected worlds. In the seasons where I've chosen holiness over grace, I've found that choosing to pursue holiness alone is never enough. When I start to think about living upright and pleasing the Lord, and I forget about grace, I am never enough. I am never up to par. I can never quite live up to the picture of holiness in my head.

And when we swing toward grace and away from holiness,

things get murky and dangerous in a whole new way. When we talk about grace without holiness, grace begins to lose its weight. If God isn't holy and hasn't made us holy, then sin isn't such a big deal, grace isn't so necessary, and it's a lot easier to dole out grace to one another. The only problem is, this easy come and easy go grace is empty—we can never seem to get enough of it, because it doesn't change us or spur us on to a better way. And when we've forgotten God's holiness and our own holy standing, which He so freely gives, we don't remember how much we need grace, so we certainly don't remember to give it to others. Grace without holiness fails us, leaves us wanting more, leaves us asking, *Is this all there is?*

The symptoms of forsaking holiness in my own life look like rhythms of constantly treating myself, excusing myself, and becoming desensitized to the things of this world that break God's heart. I forget that I was sent here to be the light in the dark, not to learn to love the dark myself. When I swing too far into grace without embracing holiness, I give up easily and early, without pressing in and pushing forward into the abundant fruit God has for me. I find myself defending my own sin and judging everyone else's, and screaming at the world, "I need a break! Give me some grace! Don't you see I'm trying over here?!" Grace without holiness doesn't satiate. It doesn't solve my problems.

Here's the thing. As I began to wrestle with God in this tension, He brought a wild possibility to mind: What if grace and holiness were never meant to work at odds with each other? What if God has always intended for grace and holiness to work *together* in gorgeous harmony?

What if God has always intended for you to dance in grace, stand on holy ground, and run on mission?

Can you imagine? If we put aside our struggles and stepped into a new way as a woman called to dance, stand, and run? Sure, it's messier and far more mysterious than an either/or, grace-or-holiness lifestyle. But I think that's what the abundant life looks like.

The absolute truth is that I'm not the wrong girl to write this book, and you're not the wrong girl to read it. No matter where your heart is in regard to grace and holiness, this book is for you. We *are* recipients of God's great grace, *and* we are set apart as holy daughters of God. I believe God has invited all of us to *move* in worshipful response to His glory.

It's time for the daughters of God to dance in celebration of grace, to truly grasp the freedom we have and the darkness we've been brought out of. For the sake of our own spiritual abundance and the glory of God, we get to stand firm on the holy ground that's been purchased for us by the blood of Jesus. We get to accept that when God calls us holy, that's exactly what we are, that our holiness was imparted to us through the righteousness of Christ. We get to live in a way that agrees with and affirms who He says we are. And in the name of Jesus and for the advancement of His kingdom, once we've gripped the grace He's given us by faith and planted our feet on His holy ground, we get to run on mission as ambassadors of life, hope, truth, and love.

We are the daughters of God. We get to dance in grace, stand in holiness, and run on mission. And we're ready to get started. Amen?

Chapter 1

WE'RE MISSING OUT

RECLAIMING OUR HOLY IDENTITY

Read by my sister, Caroline Hopper

I like to know where I'm going before I get there, which I feel is pretty common for most of us. No one wants to be sent to the dentist if she thought she was headed out for ice cream. And you certainly don't want to be told you're on your way to a wedding, only to arrive at a funeral. For this reason, I'm going to tell you now where we're headed so that we're all on the same page. This is a book of story and study that I'm praying leaves us all changed and shifted, with our eyes on God and our souls ready for action.

I'm a storyteller by nature, and I see so much power in sharing our testimonies and tales, connecting us to one another and the Lord all at once. So in this book, you're going to find real, true, honest stories—not tidied up or glossed over. (If we're going to talk about holiness, we have to talk about sin. And if we're going to talk about sin, we have to be real.)

But I'm also a Bible girl, a believer that our generation of women can and should dig deep into God's Word—for our joy and growth and for His glory and good pleasure. So on the back end of each chapter, we'll dive into God's story and shift our eyes to Him for some age-old wisdom.

By now you've read my Easter Sunday story, so you know I'm coming into this book humble. I'm expectant. I'm not afraid of the outcome. I'm anticipating what God will do in us as we explore these topics, but I am humbled. Please don't picture me fearlessly leading the pack into battle. I'm sitting here, fingers literally trembling, coffee-fueled, and having asked many friends to pray for me through this process. I'm not writing to wow you, astound you, or compel you with my winning words. I'm not writing because I have a story to tell or because I'm just so incredibly gifted or because the words are all in me like soldiers ready to march out. I'm writing these stories and digging into this study *with* all of you because I believe God wants to change *us*—me, you, all of us together—and use our lives to change the world. I'm less of an expert and more a friend on the same journey you are. I've gone from having my heart pricked by some hard questions to searching God's Word for answers and seeking to understand His aim for our lives.

What I've found is that we're all experts on grace and holiness if we're believers in Jesus. We're all covered in the same grace and given the same image-bearing identity. Who would you count as the expert of going to the moon? The guy who has read the most books about it or the guy who has actually gone there? Who's the expert on knitting? The lady who has watched a million YouTube videos or the one who has made a sweater?

The same is true for us. There's a temptation to believe that we're not qualified to consider these loftier spiritual concepts if we haven't studied up enough, if we haven't been to seminary or read our Bibles daily for twenty years. But that's where the ideas of grace and holiness diverge from your normal subjects of expertise, because it's not in reading or studying that we become authorities. It's in the receiving and believing that we find our identities as women who have grasped grace and been made holy. Since we're all in need of the same grace and imputed the same holy identity as image bearers of Christ, there is no margin for hierarchy or different levels of expertise. In case you didn't catch that word *imputed* in the glossary at the back of the book yet, all it means is that we've been assigned the identity of Christ. His righteousness, His holiness, His goodness. When God looks at us, He sees Jesus.

Because I believe it's easier to follow when you know where you're going, and because I believe lots of us have different connotations rolling around in our hearts and heads regarding holiness, I want to make my case for holiness as quickly and as plainly as I can. If you've been a follower of God for decades on end, or if you're new to these ideas and concepts, I want to invite us all to read the next few sentences with awe and belief. I want to invite the Lord to help us see the whole of holiness and respond to it in worship.

Followers of Jesus believe that God is holy, meaning He is set apart and completely and utterly unlike us. He is totally good, totally righteous, totally loving and pure. He is perfect, without sin. We believe that we, in contrast, are born as humans not perfect and not pure, but rather born with hearts that stray and sin, that swing toward unrighteousness and selfish living. That's the bad news.

Here's the good news:

29

God didn't just create us to watch us fail without hope; He always had a plan to bring the hearts of His people back to Him. The plan was to send His Son, Jesus, who is fully God and fully man, to earth to die for our sins. This is what we call justice—because God can't be holy and turn a blind eye to the fact that we're not. There had to be some price paid for the trespass of our brokenness as a whole. God sent Jesus, who is also holy, to pay the price for our sin, so that there would be justice and we could have a bridge back to God—that's grace!

God comes toward us with a solution that we don't deserve and couldn't have come up with on our own. When God looks at us, He sees the righteousness of Christ, He sees Jesus's perfection. So we get to act like His kids—coming boldly to talk to Him, growing in grace and truth as we learn more about Him, and looking forward to living in paradise with Him for eternity.

That rescue plan sounds great, but it's not even the whole story. There's more good news! God didn't just make a way for us to be in relationship with Him, He also gave us new identities—so that even when we continue to be human, continue to struggle, continue to need Him—we'd still know where we stand with God. He gave us Jesus's identity—that of a holy child of God, set apart to be in community with Him and to bring other people with us. That's our holiness, our new identity.

And there's still more than just victorious rescue and abundant identity. He also gave us jobs. And gifts. And passions. He didn't just allow us into the kingdom—He gave us the ability to use the individualized personalities, talents, and stories we possess to partner with Him in telling as many people about this amazing news as we can. That's mission.

So, friend! If you stayed with me through all of that, here

is what this means for you and me: if by grace we have faith in Jesus, *we are already holy*. Look down at your feet, look around at your home, and take a long glance at your life as it is now: you're on holy ground.

If you have the identity of Jesus written over your life, you cannot become more holy, you cannot grow to be more holy, you cannot act more holy. You just are. Already.

So what's this book even about, if we're already holy? And what if you don't feel holy right now? What if your life doesn't look holy right now? What if you see other believers or churches living in a way that sure doesn't seem holy to you?

Here's the deal: God made us holy when He sent Jesus to die for us and give us a new identity. BUT! The Holy Spirit gets in on the action throughout the rest of our lives when He teaches us in the same gracious way to agree with our holiness. God has already decided we are holy like Him; He's already done the work to make it so. The only question here is: Will we agree with that proclamation over our lives, and will we say yes to the work the Holy Spirit wants to do in us to make us more like Jesus?

First Peter 1:14–16 says it this way: "As obedient children, do not conform to the evil desires you had when you lived in ignorance. But just as he who called you is holy, so be holy in all you do; for it is written, 'Be holy, because I am holy.'"

If all of the New Testament is telling us we need God and can't work our way to Him, surely He wouldn't tell us to become holy without His help. No, He does the heavy lifting (by sending Jesus and offering us grace) and we do the agreeing—with our lives, our days, our spare time, our decisions, our relationships—by the power of the Holy Spirit. The incredible act of being holy, for us, is one of acknowledgment and confirmation when we allow the miraculous work of sanctification, of God making us more like His Son.

I love how Ephesians 2:7–10, *The Message* version, puts this:

Now God has us where he wants us, with all the time in this world and the next to shower grace and kindness upon us in Christ Jesus. Saving is all his idea, and all his work. All we do is trust him enough to let him do it. It's God's gift from start to finish! We don't play the major role. If we did, we'd probably go around bragging that we'd done the whole thing! No, we neither make nor save ourselves. God does both the making and saving. He creates each of us by Christ Jesus to join him in the work he does, the good work he has gotten ready for us to do, work we had better be doing.

Did you hear that? Our salvation is God's gift from start to finish. We're all equal recipients. So this book is a conversation from one gal to another, exploring what it's like to be spared from darkness, brought into marvelous light, made new in Him, called to consecrated living, and set free to run on mission. It's a reminder for us to look down at our feet, see where we stand with God, and to allow the holy truths He's written over our lives to compel us forward. It's not a book to "should" us into something we're not, but rather a book to help us recall *who we already are*, who God has already named us, in Christ alone.

I pray that after we recall, we'll continue to grow in our agreement with the Holy Spirit as our lives become even more filled to the brim with the holy moves of women who know that God has firmly planted them on holy ground with a purpose.

I'd love to just pause here and pray with you all if that's okay. Will you pray too? Add on to my words or just pray them for yourself, whatever feels right:

Father, we only care about this because we care about You. Because as Your girls, Your daughters, we want to know how to walk right with You—how to soak up Your grace and Your love, how to stand in the holiness that accompanies relationship with You, and how to run on mission into the world with the good news of the gospel. But real talk, God, this subject is funky. Over the years, a lot of us have been told crazy stuff, and we've believed slightly misleading information. Some of us have been digging for truth, and some of us have been scared to look too closely at what Your Word says about this, scared it will shift us more than we're willing to be shifted. But we're ready now to open our eyes and open our hearts. You're worth it, and we need Your help.

We're not scared, but we're humbled. Humble us more. Remind us of who is King, and remind us that you are the prize.

Holy Spirit, be gentle and complete. Work in our hearts and change us. Send us out. Keep condemnation and confusion far from us. Help us to read with eyes to see conviction for only ourselves, and give us blinders to the issues of our sisters and friends. We don't want to be reading with anyone else in mind but You—Your character, Your love, and Your glory. We're here and we're ready to dance, stand, and run. We love You. Do Your thing.

In Jesus's good and holy name, amen.

MY STORY: THE HOLY HUNGER

My spiritual story follows an arc that I'm finding is not atypical for women in my generation. I met Jesus at fifteen and spent a few years hiding. I hid my secret sins and my habits and my real thoughts and fears, because I wanted to appear holy. I hid my smoking, drinking, and some of the normal teenage no-no's, but I also hid the brokenness in my heart that led me to those things.

In those days, you wouldn't have heard me talk about body insecurity or feeling like I never measured up. I certainly wouldn't have shared that I was positive I was the messiest and most busted girl anyone ever knew, emotionally and physically. I kept all of that hidden and locked away, which meant I didn't have to be ashamed of my issues. As long as the outside of my life looked tidy, no one seemed too concerned that my insides might have some serious structural damage.

A few years after coming to know Jesus, I decided to "get serious" about my faith. My days and nights became all about ministry, and my identity became wrapped up in the things I could *do* for God. Not only did I continue to keep the secret sins and shame buried deep inside me, but I also began to serve at every single opportunity and try to out-read Beth Moore when it came to the Bible. I didn't know how much of the Bible Beth read each day, so I just guesstimated and tried to beat her, because that's what it takes to be holy, right? I was doing whatever I perceived it took to become "holy." For me that looked like working for holiness by trying to seem holier than the holiest person I knew.

But everything changed when I encountered grace and the true meaning of the gospel. My soul took a deep breath for the first time when I was enveloped by the liberty of our loving Jesus.

I discovered I didn't have to earn any kind of standing or holiness for God. In fact, I couldn't. Here's how that happened:

I was twenty-five, had three children, and had been in ministry for years when my husband literally sat me down and gently explained the gospel to me. He explained that my sins had already been forgiven—not just my past sins, but my present and future ones as well. He told me that the bad news was that I was not enough on my own, but the *good news* was that Jesus was enough and He loved me, lived inside me, and wanted good for me.

He lovingly told me it was a good start that I believed the gospel, but I could also *receive it* for myself. I could stop hiding all my sins to try and fit in, and I could stop trying to *serve my way* to God. For the first time in my life, I *got* grace. And for the most part, I felt the freedom to quit pretending like I had it all together. I felt safe to live as a daughter of God, to bring my whole self and story to the table, to walk in the identity of an ambassador and not an orphan who was desperately trying to earn her keep, to allow my hidden, inner wounds to receive the healing and life-changing light of Christ.

The changes were nuanced but real. My life might not have looked much different on the outside, but on the inside it was like I could see color for the first time. The idea that I could let go of the death-grip I had on "How is God perceiving me?" and instead allow Him to love me—it made my soul soar. I had thought I had signed up for a lifelong pursuit of earning my Jesus badge, when suddenly I realized He'd already stamped approval all over me and covered me in a banner of endorsement, just as I am, through the power of the cross and the resurrection.

I began to loosen up on some of the practices that I had believed kept me walking toward holiness. I stopped teaching my (toddler-aged) kids dozens and dozens of Scripture verses. I stopped waking up freakishly early to read the Bible. I stopped saying yes to every single opportunity to serve. I stopped obsessively listening to sermons by multiple pastors and reading *Systematic Theology* like it was a magazine. For the first time in a long time, I picked up easy beach novels and began watching the occasional reality-TV show. I wasn't scared anymore to sing along to Adele with my kids, instead of keeping it VeggieTales only. I still served occasionally. I didn't talk as much about the difference between justification and sanctification, because I got what I believed to be the gist of the story: God was good, and He loved us. Right? Right.

I lived like that for the better part of five or six years. This inward freedom was such a beautiful thing, and I'm not telling you that it was wrong. I was giving my soul the space to long for God on its own, not pressuring it into submission with the threat of being discarded or discounted.

The problem for me was an equation one. I'm not much of a math girl, but I am a linear-logistical thinker and this is how I'd describe what was going on in my soul. My old equation had been this: Holy work + Clean living + Hiding brokenness = One day be holy. My new equation, after understanding more about grace, was something like this: Occasional work + Pretty much clean living + Being more open = Comfortable Christianity. I was unclear about where holiness came in, God's holiness or mine. I certainly didn't feel holy, but I also didn't feel the need to work for that favor with God anymore.

I felt relief from the lack of striving, but there was something else there too. My contentment with comfortable Christianity let me off the hook with its grace, but I wasn't sure what it *led* to. What was the point of it? My equation left me empty, hungry, and still a little unsure of what I was supposed to do with myself. As the years passed, I started to believe that God might have another equation I was missing out on, one that equaled abundance and life. But I just wasn't sure what it was.

Certain activities exacerbated the ache in my heart—some you might expect and some you might not. Reading the Bible, for instance, always stirred up interesting feelings. I wanted more but I was never sure why. If I was off the hook and didn't need to work my way to God, was it condemnation and striving in my heart that left me craving more wisdom? Surely not, but I wasn't sure what the alternative was. I'd leave coffee dates with friends, feeling empty and achy for talk about eternity. I didn't want to slip back into uber-spiritual-working-her-way-to-Jesus-Jess, but I wished we'd talked more about the kingdom. Or maybe we had talked about church and serving and ministry, but I'd wish we had just talked to God together.

I'd feel the ache when I self-soothed with Netflix, when group conversations turned toward gossip, or when I bypassed homeless people seemingly carelessly. Some of the activities that left me feeling the holy ache weren't necessarily wrong, but with my current equation, there wasn't a clear-cut answer about what to do with these activities. I noticed that many of my friends felt unsure how our casual Christian community equation applied to different areas of our lives. We were free from the burden to live perfectly, and even encouraged in our transparency, but there were no clear lines for us to follow anymore. What should we do about alcohol? How much should we study the Bible? Is it okay to cuss occasionally? How much should we be serving? What about nice houses and cars? Are those okay? Where do we land about debt when we're not living in shame anymore?

There was a definite ache, a hunger to understand where this was all heading, and a desire in my heart to experience an equation that took God's holiness into consideration and gave me a clear-cut path to where that holiness intersected with my life.

It was as if the Spirit inside me was getting mouthier, crying out: "*This* is what you're meant for. Sure you have the freedom and the grace to live inside blurred lines, but just because you were freed from working for your place in the kingdom, you're not removed from it. You were saved from sin and set apart for more." When I was trying to work my way to God, the path was clear. But now that grace had entered the picture, what path was I on? What was the end goal? How did I get there? I was aching to pursue holiness but didn't know where to find it within the confines of my grace-based faith.

I didn't yet understand that our faith is a wondrous one that holds these realities in tension: grace and truth, forgiveness and holiness. For so much of my life, I *thought* I had to pick a team. I didn't realize they could coexist beautifully, just as God always intended.

Flashing back to that Monday after my somber Easter morning, all of these notions and ideas were swirling in my heart and head as the Holy Spirit started sorting out some serious paths to understanding for me. I was beginning to see a new equation, one that started with God's holiness and ended with mine. It looked more like this: God's holiness + Jesus's sacrifice = a new identity based on grace *and* holiness.

I was starting to perceive that I could accomplish my continual acceptance of grace while still standing firm on holy ground. And when I embraced the pardon that Jesus was offering and acknowledged the sacred, sanctified life He was leading me to, abundant life was mine for the taking. More than that, if I could champion both grace and holiness, others might be spurred on, encouraged, and they might want to join me in this marvelous light.

My mind was spinning with fresh explosions of understanding that morning, and I needed to chart my thoughts. Here's what I knew to be true:

Somewhere along the way, I traded my pursuit of God for a casual acceptance of God's grace. I failed to make the connection in my heart that grace spurs us on to holy living when I stopped trying to live holy in an effort to be accepted. It hurts my heart (and maybe my pride) to say I accepted it casually, but I know it's the most honest thing I can say. What I'm realizing now is that without a sobering and continual look at sin and holiness, we can't truly grasp how great grace is.

This cycle of perceiving God's holiness, needing His grace, and standing firm in the holiness He imparts to me is one I'll be participating in for the rest of my life. He won't stop being righteous and otherworldly; I won't stop being dependent on His forgiveness, and I'll always need to be looking down at where He has placed me to remember who I am and where I stand.

If God's Word is true, then my sin is vast and separates me from God's perfection, or His holiness. But because of grace, I'm not only forgiven—I'm made holy like Him.

Through Christ, God's holiness was imparted to me, and my actions and my life were no longer about earning that holiness, but about responding to it in gratitude and obedience. I wanted a life that agreed with and affirmed what God intended for me, but I no longer needed to strive in an attempt to become what He'd already made me.

Looking at all of these truths and dwelling on them compelled me to tell others what I'd found. If there is the opportunity for us to miss these foundational truths, even inside the church, I wanted to help remind the women all around me of what God has spoken over our lives. Moreover, I saw signs of women believing some of the same misconceptions I had: that grace was easy and cheap, not all that much to behold. I saw them believing that all of life was a path to becoming more holy, rather than standing in the truth that they already *are* holy and all of their days are an opportunity to agree with what God has said about them. It seemed that because of this, many women around me perceived mission as something they had to do or something they were potentially exempt from, rather than a beautiful privilege to share the truth they'd so miraculously received.

What I want you to hear most is this: If we could see the fullness of our sin and the depth of His grace, we'd dance. If we knew our true identity as holy daughters of God, made right with Him and called to stay set apart for His glory and our abundance, we'd stand firm. And if we fully grasped both of these things, you wouldn't be able to stop the women of God from running on mission.

All this came from three, minute-long conversations about a silly teenage TV show. God sure works in miraculous ways, amen? Second Corinthians 5:14 was ringing in my head that morning. It tells us that "Christ's love compels us, because we are convinced that one died for all, and therefore all died." Sitting and sipping my coffee, I felt the sobering realization that in *my* personal experience, I'd let the love of Christ compel me to continually thank Him for grace, but that was about it. I didn't let it compel me to change. God's forgiveness wasn't meant to be a numbing agent that tranquilized me, absolving me from seeking after the things that please God. It took me a minute to realize that I could put down the belief that I had to please God to be loved by Him and pick up the more nuanced truth that *because God first loved me*, I might *want to* live in a way that pleases Him. God's grace is too powerful to let the transformation stop short at thanksgiving, before going back to life as usual.

I wondered if it wasn't just me who was getting tripped up in this equation, this idea that I need not be working to become a better person but that I merely needed to agree, or become who God has already made me to be. As I was feeling the weight of hiding my holiness, it wasn't that I was feeling convicted for not being good enough but that I was feeling the anguish of not being *myself*.

So that's where I sat on the Monday after Easter 2016. I was feeling the burden of having forgotten holiness. I was realizing that my head knew the truth—that I stood on holy ground as a daughter of God—but my heart was having a hard time catching up. I wanted to understand how and why I had gotten to this spot, starting with when I began to believe in grace instead of receiving it and when I had given up the pursuit for consecrated Christlikeness.

THE MAIN POINT IS THIS:
WE'RE MISSING OUT

The truth I was missing all those years is that my faith life is not a two-party system. We don't have to *choose* between pursuing holiness and celebrating the grace we've been given. Instead, we're invited into abundant life—grace and holiness in harmony together. Can I repeat that again with some emphasis? We don't have to *choose* between standing on holy ground and dancing in grace; we *get* to do both all at once. No one is saying we *must* live a different way, and you won't hear the word *should* come out of my mouth in this context either. I'm not passionate about this message because I believe we're doing it all wrong. I'm passionate about this message because I think that without it, we're missing out on the abundant life we most crave.

As much as this is a "get to," there's still some tension for those of us who realize this isn't the truth we live in our day-to-day lives. I'd love for us to sit now, holding that tension, aware that something is amiss among the daughters of God, that something has gone awry. Perhaps you're like me, and you feel it strongest within yourself. Maybe it's an ache you've carried for your sisters in Christ—you've longed to see them understand grace *and* truth, holiness *and* liberty. Maybe you just feel the tenderness for all of us, the sisters and the wild women of God across the world—the ones with the heaving and heavy hearts who have longed to feel at ease in their identities and in their relationships with the Lord.

Wherever you sit, I invite you to hold that ache and look to the possibility of grace and holiness working together in our lives— because it is going to be essential to our hope moving forward.

My favorite pastor (my husband, Nick) illustrates abundance for me in a way that makes me yearn for more, more, more of Jesus. I feel like Alice in Wonderland peering over the edge of the rabbit hole, ready to cannonball in and get lost in the mystery of all that He is. Nick describes abundance as being convinced that we have all that we could ever need, want, or desire because we have Jesus. It's true that our God supplies what we need and meets the desires of our hearts, but abundance is about so much more than that. Abundance is rooted in the undeniable and inexhaustible truth that God supplies all we need just by giving us His Son, Jesus. We'll dive down this rabbit hole in later chapters, but suffice it to say here that when we accept God's grace without acknowledging His incredible holiness, we don't see the full, abundant, miraculous nature of this relationship we've been pulled into.

Rather than being women who are slowly becoming likened to the status quo that surrounds us, grasping grace and standing our holy ground enables us to change the world—not be changed by it. It's not that God needs us to get this; it's that we *get to* try and grasp it so that we can taste and see Him and share Him more effectively—experiencing more of Him here on earth than we would otherwise.

The point is, we're missing out. If we're *only* talking about grace, not receiving it and embracing it, we're not experiencing abundance. And if our faith lives are built on an assumption that we've got to work to become more holy so that we can experience grace, we're just as lost. It's in the celebration of grace *coupled with* the awareness that we've already been given holy standing with God that we start to taste the fullness of our identities. This is where it gets good, friends.

For the rest of this book, you're going to see that I don't just want you to take my word for it. These principles, these ideas about grace, holiness, and mission didn't originate with me, and as women of God, we *get to* hold our ideas up to the Bible to make sure we're on the right page and chasing the right questions. Will you join me as we dig into some other people's stories and some wisdom straight from God?

Let's Study the Word:
DANIEL 1:8–21

But Daniel resolved not to defile himself with the royal food and wine, and he asked the chief official for permission not to defile himself this way. Now God had caused the official to show favor and compassion to Daniel, but the official told Daniel, "I am afraid of my lord the king, who has assigned your food and drink. Why should he see you looking worse than the other young men your age? The king would then have my head because of you."

Daniel then said to the guard whom the chief official had appointed over Daniel, Hananiah, Mishael and Azariah, "Please test your servants for ten days: Give us nothing but vegetables to eat and water to drink. Then compare our appearance with that of the young men who eat the royal food, and treat your servants in accordance with what you see." So he agreed to this and tested them for ten days.

At the end of the ten days they looked healthier and better nourished than any of the young men who ate the royal food. So the guard took away their choice food and the wine they were to drink and gave them vegetables instead.

To these four young men God gave knowledge and understanding of all kinds of literature and learning. And Daniel could understand visions and dreams of all kinds.

At the end of the time set by the king to bring them into his service, the chief official presented them to Nebuchadnezzar. The king talked with them, and he found none equal to Daniel, Hananiah, Mishael and Azariah; so

they entered the king's service. In every matter of wisdom
and understanding about which the king questioned them,
he found them ten times better than all the magicians and
enchanters in his whole kingdom.

And Daniel remained there until the first year of King
Cyrus.

Daniel was just a kid. Scholars estimate that he and his friends
were in their early teenage years. Daniel was a healthy, strong
kid who didn't do anything to land himself in hot water, except
maybe be born a little wiser and taller than other kids. But he
was born into a remarkable cultural battle—a time when God's
people were in the midst of a fight between their worldly identities
and their kingdom identities, much like the world many of us
found ourselves born into—like we're seeing our kids born into
as well.

Daniel was the author of the book (but not necessarily the
hero). He was born an Israelite, one of God's chosen people,
in a tumultuous season, one in which other kingdoms were
fighting over who would be in charge of his people. They were
surrounded on every side by enemies and dominant governments:
the Babylonians, the Persians, the Assyrians, and the Egyptians.
Despite (or maybe because of) their hostile surroundings, the
Israelites had just undergone decades of revival under the reign
of King Josiah.

Josiah was just a boy when he became king, but as a teenager
he was a monumental player in a redemption story—God's people
returning to His Word, His covenant, His call for godly living.
This was a season of heroes of the faith emerging and saying
bold things about God. We don't see just King Josiah calling the

people back to holiness, but some major prophets also emerged in this season, namely Jeremiah and Ezekiel, who should sound familiar to us, since they have books of the Bible named after them. These were the kinds of days many of us dream of, the kinds of leaders who were written about in the greatest story ever told because their words impacted generations and nations. These books don't only detail the ministry of two rad guys; they speak life and light and Jesus to us even now—thousands of years after they were written.

So while I think the present is a pretty sweet time to be alive—we've got Beth Moore, Jennie Allen, Louie Giglio, and Francis Chan—it wasn't an uninspiring spiritual climate for Daniel either.

But then something shifted, and the first chapter of Daniel tells us that God allowed the Israelites to be given over to Babylon. King Josiah was killed in battle by an Egyptian king, who then appointed one of Josiah's sons, Jehoiakim, to be king. Jehoiakim was not the hero his dad had been. In fact, we see other biblical texts basically decrying him to be a godless, maniacal leader who weakly partnered with other kingdoms and handed over the people and products of his nation. He lived in incestuous relationships with his female relatives and basically was just an all-around bad dude.

Jehoiakim was a bad guy, the worst of the worst. He let the Babylonians come take the treasures of the people of God, and in the thick of all this drama, they took captive some of the young, noble, strong Israelite boys. The boys, who had just lived through revival and spiritual vibrance, were forced to leave their homes and families and were taken to Babylon to be made less Israelite and more worldly. The king wanted them to learn the Babylonian way—the language, the literature, and the opulence—for at least three years, at which point they'd become the king's servants.

Daniel and his pals were up against an interesting dilemma: How did they live under the rule of the king of their country while still honoring the King of their hearts? We could dig into Daniel for chapters upon chapters, but there are just a few things I want us to grab from this short passage.

HOLINESS PRACTICES A SIMPLE *YES* AND A SIMPLE *NO*

What we see was that Daniel embodied the clichéd but helpful, "Be in the world but not of the world." He said yes to going where he was taken. He said yes to the government, yes to learning. He said yes to being among people who were nothing like him. He didn't reject the people who did things that didn't honor God—he simply rejected the godless practices that would defile *him*. Daniel said yes to being in the world.

If I'm being honest, this is where the wheels get shaky for the women of God. It seems simple on paper, but it's much tougher to live out. We seem to be okay with one or the other: being completely in the world and just like it *or* being completely outside of it and only interested in judging it. God's way for us seems a lot simpler: be in the world, not judging it, but don't become like it either. It's a simple idea, but I believe we should keep saying simple things until we actually do them. It's harder to say yes to being in the world while saying no to being defiled by it at the same time.

What does it look like to do this in your life? Maybe it means being in the playgroup of moms who don't know Jesus but not laughing at the unkind jokes or leading the pack demeaning other women and men. Maybe it means seeing our lost coworkers like real humans, for whom we want good things, so we're not only treating them decently but we're also pointing them to the truth and the hope that we have. For some of us, it might mean evaluating our rhythms and our hours to see if we're spending time in the wider world. Or are we surrounded only by other believers in a safety bubble?

It might mean holding off on the ranting Facebook posts, even when we're right, simply because they'd alienate and hurt the people God sent us to love and share the light with. Saying yes to the world and no to compromising ourselves might mean saying yes to the extended family dinner and no to the temptation to enter into the family conflict that ultimately isn't going to glorify God. It might mean saying yes to being in the book club and no to silently nodding when less-than-true things are being shared at club meetings. It might mean watching our modern-day celebrities and praying for them instead of bashing them, judging them, and only using their lives as entertainment—delighting in their downfalls or puffing ourselves up with pride as if we're better than they are.

I believe it's time for the women of God to return to the simple yes and no—yes to being with the world, no to joining in its sin. Not everything is clear-cut and easy to discern all the time—some decisions are gray, and some relationships are murky. But our God is not a God of confusion, and He's given us the gift of the Holy Spirit to continually increase our capacity to discern what it looks like to live in the world without being exactly like it. As we look at Daniel's story and our own lives, however, it seems clear that there is an open invitation to dance, stand, and run by saying yes to being with people and saying no to compromising ourselves in the midst of it all.

HOLINESS LOOKS TO GOD'S FAVOR ABOVE ALL ELSE

Do you know what the name Daniel means? "God is my judge." Maybe you hear that and think it sounds pretty stern—like he's saying it with his chin tilted upwardly just so, eyes on heaven, proud and tough. But that's not the picture we see of Daniel at all. We don't see him shouting at people or carrying picket signs, even later on in the book when he has to continually give hard news and interpret tough dreams. One of the themes of Daniel's story is that he continually looks to God for how he is supposed to live, and people are impacted by *that*, not by his decrees and declarations of how everyone else is supposed to behave.

So can we own this for a moment? This, perhaps, is another area where we've gone astray as the body of Christ. We seem to swing wildly between two camps: declaring what is right and holy for the rest of the world *or* shrinking back and timidly acting as if there is no right or wrong for any of us. The story of Daniel shows us another way.

What would it look like for Christian women to say, "God is my judge. Only God. I will listen to Him and His Word and let His statutes and wisdom direct my steps, but I won't spend my life carrying the belief that it's my right or my place to worry about how God is judging others."

What I think it would look like is this: Favor. Being winsome. Living healthier. Abundant life. Lightness. Here's what we see for Daniel: When he did as God asked him to, it went better for him! His life proved that the rules and ideologies of God aren't about keeping us locked up or trapped under His thumb. The ways of God are for our *good*, for our benefit, for wisdom in and favor with the world.

If the women of God danced in grace, stood their holy ground, and ran on mission, allowing only God to be their judge, we'd find people lining up to ask about the secret behind our thriving. You remember in 1 Peter 3:15, where it tells us to always be prepared with an answer for the hope that we have? How in the actual world can we be praying for that when we are not acting as if we have hope? How can we answer if we're not acting as if we believe God is in control? First Peter 2:9 says that we're a royal priesthood and a holy nation, chosen so that we may declare the praises of Him who brought us out of darkness and into wonderful, marvelous light.

It seems to me that Daniel continually found favor with the people around him, people who wanted the light he had *because* he chose to walk in God's will. He took God at His Word and tried His way, and the result was that others wanted to know more about God.

Let's put to bed the lie that we need to live out our faith in a more palatable way for the good of the nonbelievers around us. Let's stop believing that if we make everyone else feel comfortable by dimming the light of our vibrant faith, they'll be stirred and called up to join us in belief. Let's stop judging and condemning those around us if they haven't decided they're under the authority of God, but let's not believe the author of lies when he tells us that we need to tone it down to minister well.

I have a friend whose husband was on the path to salvation, but not in a relationship with the Lord *yet*. We were praying for him to love Jesus and all the while inviting him into our community. One day, my friend and I were discussing her fear of letting him see her worship freely, lifting her hands and crying during corporate worship in church. She didn't want to freak him out, right? He didn't even believe in God. As we talked about it that day, I encouraged her to run full out after God and keep begging God to grab her husband's heart. That way, when he did decide to place his trust in Jesus, he'd know from the get-go what a passionate follower of Christ looks like. He'd know what abundance awaited him in intimacy with God. Wouldn't you know, a few months later, she walked in on him doing the dishes—worship music blaring, hands in the air, singing his heart out to God?

God is in control, and He will bring the favor. It's not on our shoulders to please or delight the world around us so that we can win people to Jesus. And it's not our responsibility to correct and judge them, since that will surely drive them away from the light. God is our judge. His way is perfect. When we dance in grace and stand our holy ground, He brings the favor and the fruit.

WE CAN BELONG, OR WE CAN BE USED

You can sit with us.

You belong.

Your story matters.

There's a place at the table for you.

These are some of the encouraging messages smattered on shirts and coffee mugs and journals in all the Christian stores in all the states. I won't lie—I've got a few of the shirts, and I like them. These messages are beautiful and helpful, and I believe during this space in history, when so many young women are unsure of their place and their worth, the encouragement is welcome. We have the joy of welcoming all the people, telling them they have a place with us, hearing one another's stories, and allowing God to use them for His glory. We get to be people with overflowing tables and open hands, not crossed arms and saved seats.

The great news of the gospel is that as women of God, we *never* have to walk into a room praying someone saved us a seat. Our souls crave belonging because God made us this way, and He's the One who gives us our belonging. We're not meant to find our place or our inclusion in the world. Our "spot" in eternity was paid for by the cross of Jesus Christ. There is more here available for us than belonging in this world and our current culture.

Our friend Daniel did not bend to fit in because he needed to belong. Instead, he chose to stand firm in order to be used. I don't like the feeling of being left out any more than the next girl. In fact, I *hate* feeling left out. I despise the sensation that everyone else has the upper hand or that they have things figured out and I don't. I don't love knowing I'm excluded, and I certainly don't want to be discounted from my community because of my faith in Jesus. Let's be real: this doesn't sound fun to anyone.

But more than I want to belong, I want to be used. And when I approach a people group—whether it's the women at my church, the other moms at my kids' school, or the gals I work out with at the gym—I don't want to feel like I need their approval when I already have all the approval I need from Jesus.

I don't want to ask other humans to fill up the gaps in my soul. Rather, I want to be taking the soul answer to them: Jesus. If we're going to change the world and stop being changed by it, we're going to have to acknowledge that we already belong, we already have a place, and we're already accepted. Not by humans or community or the kind gals we do life with, but by Jesus.

Remember in 1 Peter 1 when we were told to be holy as God is? Here's some wisdom on seeking to belong versus being used by God from the same chapter: "Since you call on a Father who judges each person's work impartially, live out your time as foreigners here in reverent fear" (1 Peter 1:17).

I also love Hebrews 13:14, which says, "For here we do not have an enduring city, but we are looking for the city that is to come." Looking down at our feet and finding ourselves on holy ground changes what we see when we look at the world around us. We stop looking at this city, this community, this world as our home, and we start remembering that we don't just find our identity in God, but that we find our future in His kingdom. We already belong, and we are so ready to be used to bring other people with us.

Women of God, I have a question for you: Are we ready to change the story?

Are we ready to wholeheartedly embrace the grace of God and reject the desire to belong to this world since we belong to the kingdom? Are we ready to take back some ground we may have given up when we lost sight of our holy standing? Are we ready to allow God to use us to change the world? Are we ready to move into this kingdom on mission, with our hearts more intent on loving others and sharing His marvelous light? Are we ready to dance, stand, and run—for the glory of God and for the sake of the world?

I know we are. Let's go.

Let's Take It a Little Further

1. What immediately comes to mind when you read Daniel 1:8? Are there areas of your life where you've resolved not to be defiled or compromised? Are there areas where you've lost some ground?

2. Proverbs 3:1–4 says, "My son, do not forget my teaching, but keep my commands in your heart, for they will prolong your life many years and bring you peace and prosperity. Let love and faithfulness never leave you; bind them around your neck, write them on the tablet of your heart. Then you will win favor and a good name in the sight of God and man." Have you believed that to have favor with others, you had to please them? Have you believed that if you stood your holy ground and let God be the judge, you might be rejected? How do Daniel 1 and Proverbs 3 turn that thinking on its head?

3. Do you resonate with longing to belong more than longing to be used? Talk with the Lord and ask Him for some immediate action steps that would show you stand on the belief that His approval is more valuable than anyone else's.

4. Take the pulse on the presence of grace and holiness in your life. Is there one you find your heart naturally gravitates toward?

Chapter 2

DON'T YOU FEEL LIKE DANCING?

THE POWER OF REVIVAL-STARTING GRACE

Read by Gina Zeidler

You know what's fun to brainstorm? Stories about times I've needed grace.

On second thought, no. That's not fun at all to brainstorm. I mean, in theory, in the seasons where I've been given much grace, I've been thoroughly shifted and changed. But it's not felt nice. It never feels nice to be given grace, after having sat in the weight of how you've hurt someone. Picture a coffee date with a friend where one of you has messed up and hurt the other and there's some forgiveness happening. Do you want to be the one saying sorry or "I forgive you"? In my experience, when I say, "I forgive you," a warm rush of sweet fuzzies floods my soul. When I say, "I'm sorry," I feel like I've swallowed moldy sandpaper.

I could tell you about all the times I've yelled at my kids. I could tell you about the season where I stopped speaking to my best friend for a few months. You gals, my sweet friends, might be impacted by some of the more wounding things I've said to my husband and how he typically immediately gives me grace and stays married to me—but none of those feel right. I think we need to get to the real sticky stuff, that moldy sandpaper stuck to the bottom of the trashcan of my soul.

I got married first out of all my college friends, when I was just shy of twenty-one and basically a maniacal teen-bride. Engaged at nineteen, I immediately turned into one of those loony tunes who develops a meticulously organized and incredibly unrealistic "wedding binder." I can remember sitting at the church I worked for the morning after Nick proposed. I'd bought a three-ring binder on the way to work, printed out a piece of paper with our names and our wedding date, and stuck it in the front plastic sleeve. I immediately began filling that thing with my scrupulous hopes and dreams for our wedding day. We were a year out from our wedding, but that didn't stop me from writing down all the details of what the day would be like—from the flowers to the menu. I even immediately drew a diagram of which bridesmaids would stand where.

For the most part, my people indulged me. I remember one frank conversation where my mom kept repeating the phrase, *Lower your expectations*, but my friends went with me to the bridal appointments and my man-to-be debated different shades of cornflower blue until we both nearly went cross-eyed. My maid of honor, Meredith, was one of the most flexible humans there was. She shared a room with me, so she heard all the details and dove in deep, and she always agreed to go on trips with me to search for wedding dresses.

One weekend, a few weeks after Nick and I were engaged, Meredith and I borrowed Nick's car (mine was not as nice, and I was feeling fancy as a bride-to-be) and drove fast and furiously to a bridal shop near my mom's house, a whole two hours away. My driving was somewhat of a joke among our friends—how I was known for singing, talking, and multitasking behind the wheel, and this day was no exception. Meredith and I talked and laughed and carried on the whole way, not a care in the world except *wedding*. We spent the day trying on ridiculously expensive dresses that I couldn't be dissuaded from and spent the first part of our ride home debating the merits of white-white versus off-white, and sweetheart necklines versus strapless. And then something crazy happened. The details are fuzzy now—the only thing I know is that it was my fault.

Simply put: my mind wasn't on the road; it was split between the past few hours at the bridal shop and the future hours I'd be spending at the altar. I wasn't speeding—I know that only because there had been a police officer directly behind me for miles, but I think I reached toward the radio, swerved, and then overcompensated. I was excited, distracted, and probably a bit overconfident. That sordid combination of small mistakes somehow led to us spinning, spinning, spinning, across the highway at breakneck speed. I'll never forget the feeling of that spin—knowing I wanted it to stop, but terrified of what would stop us. I remember screaming out the name of Jesus, and then there was smoke and stillness.

When I opened my eyes, I saw we'd spun all the way across the highway, from the far left to the far right, finally slamming into a massive concrete overpass on the passenger side. The car was unrecognizable, dented and folded in all along the entire passenger side—all except for Meredith's seat. She was safe, but just by a few inches.

She was quicker to respond than I was, crawling across the car and out the backseat of the driver's side. I rolled out slowly, crying, in shock, landing on my hands and knees and staying there—staring at the ground and sobbing for a few minutes. Eventually I called Nick and my mom, and even though they were both hours away, it seemed like they got there instantly. The police officer who'd seen the whole event unfold rushed over and repeatedly told us how lucky we were to be alive. He was sure we'd both die as he watched us spin and spin and bounce and crash into that concrete wall.

Meredith was quiet. As my mom gave us water and Nick drove us back to college (in my car, since his was totaled), I processed and talked and relived the accident, as storytellers love to do, but Meredith continued to sit silently. I do think I told her how sorry I was, and I do think she told me it was okay. But mostly I just talked and she sat quietly.

The next morning, I called the church I worked for and told them I was sore and staying home from Sunday services, which they totally understood. Meredith quietly got dressed and went to church, and when I asked her why she didn't take a day off, she humbly and gently told me she wanted to worship the Lord and thank Him for keeping her safe.

When she and our other roommates left, I sat in our quiet college-girl house and just wept. It *was* an accident, the car wreck, but there was so much sin and selfishness piled up behind it. I'd been so incredibly selfish about the wedding, demanding everyone's time and attention. My mind was solely focused on me, what was good for me, and how I was going to feel. And it wasn't just the wedding obsession; there was something else.

I knew I was a careless driver. It was a joke among my friends until it wasn't. I'd been in a few bump-ups and we could laugh about me getting dings and nicks in my car, but this wasn't that. While I still wasn't sure exactly what I'd done wrong, I knew my overall casual nature about driving had played a part in this accident, and I was broken, guilty, and convicted.

A few years ago—probably at least ten years after the accident, I confessed to Meredith how defeated I still felt about what had happened, and how of all the things I've done wrong in my life, that one felt particularly monumental to me. Maybe from the outside, it didn't look like some big dramatic sin. But I knew it was my own pervasive struggle with selfishness and carelessness that could have cost her life. And you can guess that sweet Meredith gave me grace. She'd given it to me in the moment, but even years later, she told me again that it was okay and that she'd never held on to any hurt. She set me free and handed me a big dose of Jesus's love and mercy.

I'll be honest—accepting forgiveness, accepting grace from someone else, hurts my pride. It doesn't always make me feel like dancing. Because to accept grace, we first have to claim our mess and say, "Yeah, that was all me."

Maybe you feel the same. Do you feel like dancing when you think about the grace of our Father? I find that many of the women of God in our time *don't* necessarily find themselves loving the idea of grace and/or embracing it with joy. I get it, and I've been there too. But we don't have to stay in this place of reluctant acceptance when it comes to what He's offering. Let's revisit the recent history of our faith and how we've interacted with the grace of God.

THE GRACE REVIVAL

I was in my twenties when I perceived grace capturing the modern church in a new and fresh way. I wonder where you were in this timeline—if you were born into a spiritual family that embraced grace from the get-go or one where you saw the shift occurring. Maybe you're totally new to the church and this is all news to you. Whatever your roots, get some popcorn and enjoy this super interesting story. This is the quick and dirty version of what took place in Protestant Christianity in the 1900s. It's going to sound like a history lesson, but it's important to look at where we've been so that we can better envision where we'll go from here.

The late 1800s saw lots of diversity in churches and Christian practices. It had been a few hundred years since the Protestant church broke off from the Catholic church during the Reformation, and the Protestant church continued to splinter into lots of denominations and theologies. There was so much new scientific and cultural exploration coming about on the heels of the Enlightenment, and the church's response was complicated. In this new mix of rising ideas, church leaders were nervous. Darwinism was spreading, Marxism, transcendentalism—you name it, things were shifting and new ideas were spreading.

Thought leaders, scientists, poets, and philosophers were getting louder, and the people were listening. But with so many competing voices, it was getting harder to tell truth from untruth. These voices weren't necessarily affirming Scripture or God's authority over culture and their lives, so naturally, the pastors were feeling a little crazy.

The early 1900s saw Christian church leaders feeling tender. All they held dear was seemingly being threatened as intellectual and cultural exploration were on the rise. The idea of fundamentalism came into play in the early 1920s—as pastors called for Christians to be ready to "do battle royale for the fundamentals." Now, a hundred years later, we see that not everyone necessarily agreed on what those fundamentals were or what it looked like to "do battle"—but all kinds of varying forms of the evangelical church emerged. The fundamentalists held fast to biblical truth (yay!), but also got a bad reputation for being militant and unwilling to cooperate with anyone outside their belief system (not yay).

Simply put: a line was drawn. The fundamentalists seemed to be saying, *We're over here and you're over there. We're the holy people of God, and we believe this truth. If you're with us, good. If you're not, we're going to defend our worldview and we're not terribly concerned if that offends you.* And of course, we know this isn't a message that's true for every individual in the entire movement, but it's the sentiment the outside world was left with. And this is a sentiment that I think most of us can agree leaves us feeling sad and broken for those who heard they didn't belong in the church, amen?

But there was good news! While the fundamentalist voices were loud, there were new leaders emerging who sang a song of freedom and grace to the masses, who desperately needed to hear it. There were lots of incredible, evangelistic, bold leaders preaching grace across America, but I saw the work of one of them fairly clearly because of where I grew up. One of those wild crusading, gospel-slinging preachers who came onto the scene and brought revival into the church with him was Billy Graham. From the moment he burst onto the national scene, Billy Graham was all about grace.

I grew up in Charlotte, North Carolina, near Billy's birthplace, so by the time I was paying attention, our state had entire highways named after him. I went to my first Billy Graham crusade when I was eleven, and I'll never forget what it looked like to see thousands of people rush down the stadium aisles to the stage. Not to see Billy or touch him, but to receive the gift of salvation that is offered in Jesus Christ. That's a beautiful picture, right? According to his staff, an estimated three million-PLUS people have responded to the call of salvation via his ministry. Whoosh, that's beautiful.

Billy grew up in the midst of fundamentalism and attended fundamentalist schools but departed from the movement early in his ministry because he was seeing the benefit of cooperation with other Christians and longed to see a relationship develop between the secular world and the truth of the gospel. His ministry was directed toward the masses, but also toward the secular leaders of the day—presidents, movie stars, civil rights leaders, and world politicians.

Billy was just one of the leaders in this iconic season of the American faith. There were some who came before him and many who came after him. There were well-known leaders who led thousands to grace, and God knows there were thousands of unseen gospel laborers working around the country to fight the condemnation and legalism that crept in with fundamentalism.

I wonder if in your mind's eye you can see it too. Grandmothers singing "Amazing Grace" to their grandchildren, with tears welling in their eyes as they thought on the pardon they'd received in Jesus's name. Can you picture the small churches all around America, pastors reading and re-reading Romans 11:6: "And if by grace, then it cannot be based on works; if it were, grace would no longer be grace"? Can you picture them crawling into bed beside their wives, weighing the words they've read with the culture that had already been created, wondering if Christian community might not be as rule-based as they'd always imagined?

America was seeing the roots of the Grace Revival beginning to appear—the church was growing less fearful of the outside world and more inviting to the masses. We began to see the arrival of contemporary services, pastors taking off their robes, guitars used in worship instead of organs, and hymnbooks traded for catchy choruses. This is the developing church I grew up in—one that made the transition from Sunday school to small groups. And these were just the outward manifestations of what was happening inwardly in the church. There was a pulsating push toward grace and the idea that salvation was for everyone, whether you were church folks or not. Keeping the faith was no longer widely understood as a battle against culture, but as an invitation to all.

Over the series of a few decades, it seemed like a large population of the evangelical church was swallowing whole the idea of a consistent and changing grace. Gone was the "get saved and get cleaned up so we can fight the other side" mentality. And it was beautiful! We saw words like *gospel* and *missional* and *authentic* emerging in the language of the children of God, and as a result, many communities began to hear less about *sanctification* and *consecration* and *righteousness*.

This grace was shifting our church, changing hearts and churches in varying ways. Maybe some churches kept their pews and hymnals but felt the fresh wind of freedom blowing in other ways. Still other churches may have adopted the new, more lenient cultural policies while their doctrine stayed the same. Some churches changed on the outside, some changed on the inside, some changed on both fronts. The truth remains that many were drawn back to the heart of God, and many were drawn back to the church, since it wasn't seemingly as stodgy and formal as it had been under the rule of fundamentalism.

People called it a grace revival, but I'm curious if you feel like you're living in the midst of revival right now. *What exactly is revival-starting grace?* Where we sit now, as women of God, do we know what this massive force is that has shaped our churches and our ideologies? Can we define it? Can we trace its power in our lives? Is it a phrase too familiar? Has it lost its weight? Let's do a quick refresher on this extravagant grace that has shifted our personal eternities and our collective church.

WHAT IS GRACE, ANYWAY?

The earliest mention of grace, the Hebrew word חֵן, is in Genesis 6:8 when God looks on Noah and responds to him in the midst of a wicked generation. Here's what the Word says exactly:

> The LORD saw how great the wickedness of the human race had become on the earth, and that every inclination of the thoughts of the human heart was only evil all the time. The LORD regretted that he had made human beings on the earth, and his heart was deeply troubled. So the LORD said, "I will wipe from the face of the earth the human race I have created—and with them the animals, the birds and the creatures that move along the ground—for I regret that I have made them." But Noah found favor in the eyes of the LORD. (Genesis 6:5–8)

The word *favor* is ‏חֵן‎, or *chen* in Hebrew. The Greek counter-part that we find in the New Testament is χάρις, or *charis*. Both root words are described with the following words: lean toward, incline toward, disposed to, giving a gift or blessing. Can we take a moment with that "lean toward"? Let's look at Noah's story and see what his predicament can reveal for us regarding grace. If you're anything like me, that Greek definition already has your eyes welling up with some tears. Maybe you don't even understand why, but something about the thought of God being *inclined toward you* might feel impactful in a way you hadn't imagined.

Back to Noah. This whole earth is busted and everyone is wicked. God is sad that He made man. Sin is prevalent, and this is remarkable and worth noticing for one important reason. For *grace* to be extended, for God to do His incredible leaning thing, sin and brokenness must first be present. The whole earth is messed up and God's heart is troubled, and because He is good and just, He acts in a way to right what is wronged.

But first—He leans in. He makes a way. Not just for Noah, but for the rest of creation. He initiates a solution to a problem that is our sin. Grace is God's grand gesture to draw us close to Him, because we in our sin would not make that move on our own. Grace is the leaning in of God toward our broken state. We *need* grace because our natural state as fallen humans calls for condemnation, not closeness. We deserve punishment, but He initiates proximity.

Romans 5:6–8, *The Message* version, says it like this:

Christ arrives right on time to make this happen. He didn't, and doesn't, wait for us to get ready. He presented himself for this sacrificial death when we were far too weak and rebellious to do anything to get ourselves ready. And even if we hadn't been so weak, we wouldn't have known what to do anyway. We can understand someone dying for a person worth dying for, and we can understand how someone good and noble could inspire us to selfless sacrifice. But God put his love on the line for us by offering his Son in sacrificial death while we were of no use whatever to him.

Listen, that's a whole lot to swallow, and some of you might need a praise break right now. I'd like to invite you to just take a second and reflect over that or journal about it or dance around. Throw your hands in the air, call your husband, or giggle if you need to. If it doesn't stir up something in your hearts, which is real, maybe just take a second and let yourself evaluate: *Have I taken this great grace for granted? Did I skip over my actual brokenness and sinful state too quickly and miss how grand a rescue Jesus pulled off when He leaned toward me?* Ask God to reveal to you where you may have made a mess and to reveal the wonder of His grace anew.

We can't feel the grace if we don't see the sin.

Noah's rescue doesn't seem so exciting either if we don't realize that God, who LOVED this world and made these creatures and called them good, was so grieved and broken over how far from Him they'd strayed, that He was willing to destroy all of them. As we dwell on this idea of grace, we find the impact of sin, and behind that we find LOVE. All of creation was premeditated by love and purpose when He made each of us intentionally and formed us with pleasure, down to every intimate detail, and proclaimed us as GOOD—that is love we can't fathom. And when we run as far as we possibly can from relationship with Him—toward independence, self-sufficiency, and what seems to be good to us—that is sin. And when, in His grief, He leans toward us again—while we're still sinners and sure to keep on running—to make a way for us to still be in a relationship with Him, just because He loves us and wants good for us and glory for Him—THAT is grace.

And how do we get that grace? Well that's another doozy. We've already acknowledged it's not when we do special or wise things. We're not born into grace, and we can't even choose it; we can only accept it. We receive grace by *faith*, meaning we take possession and consent to this merciful, loving, wonderful leaning in. We do it simply by believing in Him and the truth that He sent His Son to work this whole thing out for us. And when we grasp the incredible cost of this gift of grace, it compels us to live our whole lives in a way that says, *Jesus, thank You.*

Now God has us where he wants us, with all the time in this world and the next to shower grace and kindness upon us in Christ Jesus. Saving is all his idea, and all his work. All we do is trust him enough to let him do it. It's God's gift from start to finish! We don't play the major role. If we did, we'd probably go around bragging that we'd done the whole thing! No, we neither make nor save ourselves. God does both the making and saving. He creates each of us by Christ Jesus to join him in the work he does, the good work he has gotten ready for us to do, work we had better be doing.

But don't take any of this for granted. It was only yesterday that you outsiders to God's ways had no idea of any of this, didn't know the first thing about the way God works, hadn't the faintest idea of Christ. You knew nothing of that rich history of God's covenants and promises in Israel, hadn't a clue about what God was doing in the world at large. Now because of Christ—dying that death, shedding that blood—you who were once out of it altogether are in on everything. (Ephesians 2:7–13 MSG)

Before we move on, let's pause and get honest.

Did any of you feel tempted to skim that section? Did anyone feel tempted to brush off yet another chapter of another book telling you about grace? I will not begrudge you if you felt this part of the content a tiny bit elementary. Maybe it felt more like spiritual milk and less like the hearty meat your soul is craving.

Sister, I get it.

I want to write about deep things that no one has ever thought of just as much as you want to read those things. That sounds fun and special. But unfortunately, I believe we've got to talk about grace and understand it fully—even as mature women of God. I don't believe we're comprehending the pardon we've received and what it means for our lives. I see two clear indications that the women of God could use a refresher, starting with me.

The first major symptom I see of a community that's not dancing in grace is a prevalence of striving. Many of us are convinced we have to earn our badge through working, should-ing, and shaming. We can't soak up grace when we're running ourselves into the ground trying to be everything to everyone and meet the needs of anyone and everyone around us. We run ragged trying to prove to the world that we're enough and can handle our own junk. But the waves of obligation don't end with us; they move out from our own souls and onto those around us as we learn to put expectation and burdens on one another. But the proof is simple: none of us can keep up. That's not true grace.

We make agreements with requirements in all of our relationships. We tell the people around us that we can continue to be counted on and trusted to meet their needs, overlooking our own need for God. We believe we are capable of ruining our own lives and all the lives around us, forgetting the truth that God's grace is lavish, complex, and abounding.

We assume and assert God's disapproval over our lives, making jokes about being His problem child or about Him potentially losing His patience with us. As *if* His grace could run out or He could be taken by surprise at our capacity to sin. We do not seem to love grace and it looks as if we are so much more comfortable with the works-based system, not just for measuring our own approval—but for withstanding most of our relationships as well. That's not true grace.

Secondly, it's clear we are not totally embracing the great gift of God's grace because we are not actively being compelled to persuade others to join us in partaking of it. Here's what 2 Corinthians 5:11–15 has to say about what grace compels us to:

Since, then, we know what it is to fear the Lord, we try to persuade others. What we are is plain to God, and I hope it is also plain to your conscience. We are not trying to commend ourselves to you again, but are giving you an opportunity to take pride in us, so that you can answer those who take pride in what is seen rather than in what is in the heart. If we are "out of our mind," as some say, it is for God; if we are in our right mind, it is for you. For Christ's love compels us, because we are convinced that one died for all, and therefore all died. And he died for all, that those who live should no longer live for themselves but for him who died for them and was raised again.

Listen, y'all. I'd rather be the easygoing gal who tells you that you're all princesses of God and life is going to be a royal ball from here on out. What I have to say isn't easy, but I do believe it will lead to abundance if we'll let it sink in.

God loved us so He made us. We sinned so He made a way for us. We believe in Him and He leans in toward us and that's called grace and it is *beautiful*. But often, I fear that for so many of us women of God, much of our lives are spent wrestling with that grace and acknowledging our dependency on God. I fear that many of our times of devotion and worship are spent working to surrender to the stone-cold truth that we need Jesus and it's only by His grace that we're saved. I fear that much of our relationship with Him is shallow and transactional—asking Him for stuff and getting our hearts in a wad when He doesn't answer our prayers the way we hope for. I'm scared that some of us are going to go to heaven still fighting against the Lord, resisting His mercy, instead of receiving it and moving into mission. We don't *get* grace.

Including myself, it seems as if we're not *getting grace* in a way that is moving us forward. Sadly, I don't feel like I'm part of a generation that spends our days being so compelled by His grace that we're *running* to tell the rest of the world how good it is. I don't see us *persuading* the women around us to acknowledge the beautiful leaning in that is God our Father, coming toward our hearts with mercy. I don't see us acting out of our minds over this great love. That's not true grace.

It's not that I think we reject God's grace because we think we don't need it; it's more that I honestly think we're just numb to it. We've said the word so many times and placated one another with words like *freedom* and *forgiveness*, we might find ourselves saying, "Yes, yes! Grace! But also, we've got to work for what we need too, you know!" We don't see this effort as striving or rejection of what God is offering, but it is. When I look at this tendency in my own life and in the lives of people I love, I pause and wonder: *Why? Has the grace revival of our modern church allowed us to skip just a few steps so that we no longer have to dwell on our own sin and can thus no longer feel the enormous weight that's been lifted off our souls through the leaning in of God?*

I'm equally led to question if I've truly grasped grace when I see the truth that the times grace has led me to mission are rare. I know that true mission, true service, is best when it's a worshipful response to the pardon my own soul has experienced. But more often than not, I'm grieved to tell you, my own mission is more driven by expectations I've put on myself or condemnation from the Enemy. That's when I know I've fallen out of touch with true grace.

In an attempt to welcome all people and make our churches more accepting places, did we veer too far away from those fundamentals of theology—and thus make our grace cheap, easy, nothing to celebrate, and certainly nothing to share?

I believe God wants His girls to dance. I believe He wants us to perceive the problem of our sin but also acknowledge His gracious leaning in. I believe He wants us to take hold of what He's offering us with both hands and a massive smile on His face. I know we'll have more joy and peace and abundance if we do. And I believe that we can dance wildly in His grace *today*. Let's read about a woman who grasped grace in a way that led her to immediate mission, and let's believe, in Jesus's name, that this can be our story as well.

Let's Study the Word:

JOHN 4:4–30

Now he had to go through Samaria. So he came to a town in Samaria called Sychar, near the plot of ground Jacob had given to his son Joseph. Jacob's well was there, and Jesus, tired as he was from the journey, sat down by the well. It was about noon.

When a Samaritan woman came to draw water, Jesus said to her, "Will you give me a drink?" (His disciples had gone into the town to buy food.) The Samaritan woman said to him, "You are a Jew and I am a Samaritan woman. How can you ask me for a drink?" (For Jews do not associate with Samaritans.)

Jesus answered her, "If you knew the gift of God and who it is that asks you for a drink, you would have asked him and he would have given you living water."

"Sir," the woman said, "you have nothing to draw with and the well is deep. Where can you get this living water? Are you greater than our father Jacob, who gave us the well and drank from it himself, as did also his sons and his livestock?"

Jesus answered, "Everyone who drinks this water will be thirsty again, but whoever drinks the water I give them will never thirst. Indeed, the water I give them will become in them a spring of water welling up to eternal life."

The woman said to him, "Sir, give me this water so that I won't get thirsty and have to keep coming here to draw water."

He told her, "Go, call your husband and come back."

"I have no husband," she replied.

Jesus said to her, "You are right when you say you have no husband. The fact is, you have had five husbands, and the man you now have is not your husband. What you have just said is quite true."

"Sir," the woman said, "I can see that you are a prophet. Our ancestors worshiped on this mountain, but you Jews claim that the place where we must worship is in Jerusalem."

"Woman," Jesus replied, "believe me, a time is coming when you will worship the Father neither on this mountain nor in Jerusalem. You Samaritans worship what you do not know; we worship what we do know, for salvation is from the Jews. Yet a time is coming and has now come when the true worshipers will worship the Father in the Spirit and in truth, for they are the kind of worshipers the Father seeks. God is spirit, and his worshipers must worship in the Spirit and in truth."

The woman said, "I know that Messiah" (called Christ) "is coming. When he comes, he will explain everything to us."

Then Jesus declared, "I, the one speaking to you—I am he."

Just then his disciples returned and were surprised to find him talking with a woman. But no one asked, "What do you want?" or "Why are you talking with her?" Then, leaving her water jar, the woman went back to the town and said to the people, "Come, see a man who told me everything I ever did. Could this be the Messiah?" They came out of the town and made their way toward him.

About 1800 years have passed and we're in a whole new section of the Bible, but who do we come back to? Jacob and Joseph. Sweet full circle, huh?

Since we left the people of God near the end of Genesis in the last chapter, they've been through trials and triumphs, seasons of great clarity with God and long periods of silence from Him. They've been enslaved, they've tasted freedom, been victorious, and also lost their fair share of battles. And now, there's a new character on the scene—a lot of people are believing He's the long-awaited Messiah, but more people are just confused about what this zealot is trying to accomplish as He moves from town to town.

We find Jesus at Jacob's well, and He's about to do something that is so culturally inappropriate, it's hard to find a fitting metaphor to compare it to in our current context.

First of all, Jews didn't speak to Samaritans. This was a fight that had been festering for centuries, and at this point, it had escalated to all-out racism, mostly coming from the Jews toward the Samaritans. They had disputes about how worship should go down, and some of the arguments were important issues, but I think most historians with a heart would look back and say the Jews took it too far and not in a good way. Judea was in the south, Galilee in the north, and Samaria in the middle—and the bulk of the people Jesus was ministering to so hated the Samaritans that they'd typically make their travel longer just to go around Samaria.

Jesus doesn't play by racist rules, as we can see, and later in His ministry He makes a Samaritan the hero of one of His parables in order to continually point His people to the truth that ethnicity doesn't equate eternal safety. So He finds Himself in Samaria, and we can assume His disciples weren't happy about it.

Adding on to His rule-breaking morning of ministry, Jesus directly communicates with a woman at a time in history when that was expressly discouraged. Men didn't address other women, unless their husbands were present. We soon find out what kind of woman this gal is. Having been married multiple times and currently living with a man she's not married to, she is not regarded as Samaria's finest. With this added information, we find one more hurdle of disapproval that Jesus seems to plow straight through, as rabbis (or teachers, which Jesus was) would have been forbidden from associating with women of disreputable character.

I want us to pause right here and take a look at the main character of this true story. Jesus's love is revolutionary here!

He is bulldozing through acceptable standards and demolishing racism and generations' worth of bias. Why? Because His love is worth it. Because His truth trumps inequality every single day of the week. I want us to see Him when we read this passage, because He's the hero—in more ways than one.

IF YOU KNEW THE GIFT

If you knew. Sweet Samaritan woman, if you only knew. I'm so glad Jesus inserted this one little phrase in here, for generations of us to be encouraged and reminded that we don't naturally just *know* what we're being offered. It takes some pondering, it takes some pausing, and most of all, it takes the Lord opening our eyes to see what it is He's giving us.

Jesus tells her that if she knew the gift of God and who she was talking to, she'd be the one asking Him for a drink of what He has to offer. The word "gift" here is δωρεά, or *dorea*, and this is the first time it's used in the New Testament. It means "a free gift, without repayment." While this is the first time we encounter it, you can probably guess that it won't be the last. Of the ten other times this word is used in the New Testament, it's always referring to some eternal gift of righteousness or grace that God extends to us. My favorite reference of all is in Romans, and I'm going to share *The Message* version of this content with you below. It's a meaty read, but it's absolutely worth digging into:

> You know the story of how Adam landed us in the dilemma we're in—first sin, then death, and no one exempt from either sin or death. That sin disturbed relations with God in everything and everyone, but the extent of the disturbance was not clear until God spelled it out in detail to Moses. So death, this huge abyss separating us from God, dominated the landscape from Adam to Moses. Even those who didn't sin precisely as Adam did by disobeying a specific command of God still had to experience this termination of life, this separation from God. But Adam, who got us into this, also points ahead to the One who will get us out of it.
>
> Yet the rescuing gift is not exactly parallel to the death-dealing sin. If one man's sin put crowds of people at the dead-end abyss of separation from God, just think what God's gift poured through one man, Jesus Christ, will do! There's no comparison between that death-dealing sin and this generous, life-giving gift. The verdict on that one sin was the death sentence; the verdict on the many sins that followed was this wonderful life sentence. If death got the upper hand through one man's wrongdoing, can you imagine the breathtaking recovery life makes, sovereign life, in those

who grasp with both hands this wildly extravagant life-gift, this grand setting-everything-right, that the one man Jesus Christ provides? (Romans 5:12–17 MSG)

The reason I love this passage so much is because it grasps the *entirety* of the gift we've been given through grace by including a weighty sit-down about sin. We just can't talk about grace without talking about sin. We can't talk about what we've been pardoned from without acknowledging that we seriously need some pardoning. To be the kind of women who fully grasp this incredible gift that Jesus continually stands in front of us offering, we've got to be women who continually grasp that we're in need. And can't you just imagine that the complete message behind what Jesus was saying to the Samaritan woman and is saying to us is just that? If you knew how broken you are, if you knew how badly you really need Me, if you could see how great the divide is between your humanness and My perfect glory—then you'd see what I'm offering, and you'd beg for it.

We wouldn't shrug it off. We wouldn't try to do it on our own. We wouldn't sweep it under the rug. Just look at the story: the very next thing He does for this woman, before He declares Himself the Messiah to her and sends her off into mission—He points to her sin.

He doesn't condemn her or shame her. He doesn't tell her that she's discounted or not worthy of being near Him. His proximity to her never changes, but goodness gracious—He points it out. Jesus lets her feel the weight of her sin so that she can feel the strength of His grace.

To be women who grasp grace and give it away like this missional Samaritan gal, we're going to have to do the same.

In the loving light of a Father who wants good for us, we get to take a look at who we really are and what we're struggling with, so that the relief from our own transgressions is not just quickly ingested—but received in fullness.

I think this may be a huge game changer for our generation. It feels so important and weighty, and I don't want us to miss the invitation we have here to be women who hold grace and truth in our hands with our eyes wide open and our hearts free and clear.

If we knew the gift, oh what we'd do.

WELL, WE KNOW WHAT WE'D DO

Thankfully, we don't have to contemplate too long what our next steps would be, since our sweet Samaritan friend models the adequate response to someone who swallows whole the new life and freedom they've received. She runs. On mission. To go tell the whole town. Grace does not have to make us hang our heads in somber acceptance! Grace can make us feel JOY. The beautiful truth that we're dependent on one who is righteous and ready to make us the same can make us HAPPY, despite our circumstances, and propel us forward.

She doesn't think about her own reputation, if she'll be rejected for her former sins or discounted for her method of ministry. This passage doesn't even give us an account of her getting her act together first or cleaning up her life before she begins bringing other people to hear what Jesus has to say.

We've got to be able to be women who fully grasp the weight of our sin, the freedom of the grace we've been given, and the holy ground we've been placed on as daughters of God—and then move on to the mission God has for us. We can learn from the Samaritan woman in this, as she takes Jesus at His word, but she doesn't dwell on her own brokenness. It's not about us; He's the main character, after all. We're not hiding where we've been or what we've done or the eternal truth that we need Him and we're going to continue needing Him. Our life is not our own and neither is our story—we want His glory, and really, we want other people to come and see this man who told us all we ever did and loved us anyway.

We'll be dancing all the way there too, you can count on it.

Let's Take It a Little Further

1. Are there cultural considerations and biases that you've allowed, like the Jews of Jesus's time, to weigh heavier in your mind than that of God's declaration over His kids? Are there people you haven't given grace to that He has?

2. What are some areas of your life where you've been given grace but maybe haven't felt the joy of freedom? Do you think it's due to not truly seeing the sin you were forgiven for?

3. What would it look like in your life to count the cost of your sin without living in condemnation and shame? What would it look like to hold grace and truth in the same hand?

4. What is keeping you from dancing in grace and running to tell your friends about Jesus?

Chapter 3

DRAW A CIRCLE

WHY HOLINESS STARTS WITH YOU

Read by my ministry partner, Jensine Lee

I sat on my couch, slammed my laptop closed, and threw back my head in frustration. Facebook was ruining my life again. I know I'm being melodramatic here, but this is real talk—that's how it felt. I'd spent just a few moments scanning my news feed, and my heart was all kinds of twisty, busted, angry, and scared. I first logged on to this beautiful social media platform in college, when it was fresh and none of us were quite sure what to call it. *Bookface? The book of faces? What's happening here? Huh?*

Back then, it was refreshing and sweet to see high school friends and catch up on out-of-town relationships. I loved posting my wedding pictures on "the book," then baby pictures, then more baby pictures. For a while, it was so innocuous and enjoyable.

But something has shifted in the past few years, and I don't think I'm the only one who feels it. More and more often we're becoming "friends" with people we have no connection to, people from whom we don't even have six degrees of separation. Or maybe we do have a degree or two, but the truth remains: we don't really know these people and we're not actually in community with them. You know when this is most apparent? When people argue on Facebook. And that, friends, is what was ruining my life on this particular day. Often, when I see people Facebook bickering, I get sucked into the vortex of the angry comments, and here's the gist of what I read: "Janice! I don't know how I know you or how we got connected on here, but you're an absolute idiot and nothing you say makes sense!"

Girl, I know you've seen that comment too. Or maybe even the slightly more connected and therefore more painful, "Heather! I'm your mom's second cousin, twice removed, and I'm embarrassed to see that you would share such a stupid article. And your baby needs to put on some socks for goodness' sake. His toes are going to fall off." Tell me I'm not the only one watching these kinds of interactions go down? And please tell me you read that with a Southern accent. Because I'm super Southern and that's how I hear it in my head, even if the gal writing it is in Southern California.

So, this one day, I'd gotten sucked into the feed. As I scrolled, I realized I knew none of these people, but here I was, invested in their political stances, their religious opinions, and their kids' Halloween costumes. I couldn't look away as they essentially shouted into the wide open internet all of their positions—and today the feed was feisty. This day in particular, the book of faces was riled up and ready to go—hurling insults at one another while cutting and slashing each other's souls in the process.

And why was this ruining *my* day? Because I was born with a tender soul and can't leave well enough alone. I look like a tough cookie with my messy blonde hair and red lipstick, but inside I'm about one sweet cat video away from crying at all times.

It's the middle child in me that hates fighting and likes conflict resolution. Any conflict engagement on my part is all for the sake of reaching some sort of peace. I have a heart that pursues peace through putting all the facts and truths and hard stuff on the table, then painstakingly sorting it out with the people I love. Growing up, I was the weird kid who wanted to interrupt my parents' arguments, sure that I could help them reach some common ground since I could hear where they were misunderstanding one another. And that's why the angry voices on Facebook were messing with me that day, even though I didn't know a single face behind one of them.

With my head thrown back and my hands resting on my closed laptop, I thought about what they were all trying to say. They were trying to tell each other what was wrong with the world, and thus, what was wrong with one another. They weren't speaking encouragement, life, or truth about what was *good*, what they loved, or even what they hoped would happen to make the world a better place. They were just yelling about what they hated and what, from their perspectives, makes everything so hard here on earth.

So on that incredibly frustrating and peaceless day, I decided not to let the story I heard be told by strangers on the internet alone. It seemed that Facebook was negative and everyone there kept yelling about what they hated. But in all honesty, Facebook wasn't my enemy, and I'm typically the first person to remind others that social media *can be* another tool for sharing truth, the gospel, and the light of Christ with our world. If Facebook was going to tell me what it hated, then I needed a holy way to fight back. I couldn't just respond with the same vitriol and silliness I was seeing.

I've found that the holiest way to fight fear and anger is with truth. The truth here is that the Bible doesn't only talk about how unholy it is for humans to operate out of hate. God's Word also contrasts human hate to godly hate, giving us a glimpse again of this great divide between our brokenness and His perfection. I began to wonder what "holy hate" would even look like and if there was anything in my life that would stir that up in the Lord.

I remembered a passage about the things God hates, so I went there first, and I'd like you to head there with me now. But first I want to give you the Hebrew background of this word for "holy hate," as we're now calling it. I'm asking God to give us hearts that understand His hate is not like ours, seething with sin and brokenness, but about perfection and His inability to be mixed up in unloving or unrighteousness behavior.

Hate, שָׂנֵא (pronounced *sane*): to detest, to be an enemy of, to be foes. To turn away.

There are six things the LORD hates, seven that are detestable to him: haughty eyes, a lying tongue, hands that shed innocent blood, a heart that devises wicked schemes, feet that are quick to rush into evil, a false witness who pours out lies and a person who stirs up conflict in the community. (Proverbs 6:16–19)

I'm just going to ask that you dig in with me here and see what God has for us. I need to be honest from the get-go and tell you, too, that I feel like if I were going to make a list of what I think God hates without referencing this passage, my list might look a lot different.

I would think we'd see crooked politicians, child pornographers, modern-day slave traders, and evil dictators at the top of the list. When I picture God fuming, I picture Him fuming at those kinds of people, and it's pretty comforting to me to know that their version of evil is so overwhelmingly worse than mine—that I'm on one side of this fight and the bad guys are on the other. Until, that is, I start reading this list.

HAUGHTY EYES

The Hebrew word for haughty is רוּם, or *rum*, and it literally means higher, or raised up. It's a literally translated phrase that essentially means anytime you look down on someone or something. So let's pause. Swallow our coffee. Take a deep breath.

At the top of the list of things our God hates is something that we're all guilty of. Me. You. All of us. And let's be real—we're not talking past tense. We're not talking pre-Jesus or when you were a teen or before you got saved and got your life together. At some point today, yesterday, or this week, we all looked at someone else and thought of ourselves as higher, wiser, better, stronger, more gifted, or more righteous. I asked a few brave women on Facebook (the irony!) to go first and tell me ways they currently saw themselves as better than other people, and here were the answers I got. See if you identify with any of them:

> I think I'm better than others when I'm more in the know about things than them, have more answers than them, have more wisdom than them.

> I think I'm better than others because of how busy I stay/ how much I'm involved in.

I think I'm better than other moms when I prioritize the needs of my one-year-olds, and I see them do things I perceive as selfish.

I think I am better than people when I can easily admit I am a broken mess in need of mercy daily while others still need to keep the mess all tied up and hidden underneath a pretty little bow.

I feel better than folks I see as less educated or "misled" or just plain wrong on certain issues because I tell myself I'm wiser, better educated, or somehow better than them.

I feel I'm better than others when I manage my time well and can get lots of things accomplished even though my life is always full.

I think I'm better than other moms when I see them doing things I perceive as bad parenting.

I feel better than other people because I don't worry about the mess on the counter or dishes in the sink; also, because I can easily say no.

I think I'm better than others because I only allow them to see the "perfect" me—the perfectly packaged, tied-with-a-bow me. I act like I lead this wonderful, carefree life, when in all actuality, I'm a broke college student who struggles with time management and procrastination.

I feel like I'm better than other Christians because I'm investing in people who aren't Christians yet (or am more missional).

I think I'm better than other girls at the grocery store wearing pajamas or yoga pants because I wear real clothes and sometimes even heels.

I think I'm better than anyone who doesn't share in carrying the burdens that I carry.

Women, these are just the tip of the iceberg, right? I didn't expect my friends to lay it all out there for us to see—but you can feel it in your heart too, right? The haughty eye. In small ways and in big ways, this is us. We look down on others.

If by some crazy chance you don't relate to any of those above statements and they don't jar up any other haughty thoughts within you that you've had before, chances are you're feeling haughty toward the confessions of my friends. I say that because I'm there too. Reading them slowly and honestly, I wanted to excuse the statements I related to and I wanted to judge the ones that seemed foreign to me. My eyes are haughty. My heart is prideful. One of my biggest struggles is at the top of the list of the things God hates. Let's move on. And friends, we're just getting started. Hang in there. Let's keep going together.

A LYING TONGUE

Welp, I'll go first on this one, friends.

When I was in fifth grade, I told my entire family I met the president. There was this small sliver of potential that President Bill Clinton was going to come to my school to honor some program we'd started, and most of the school was hopeful it would happen. When the opportunity fell through, however, I made a game-time decision to lie and tell my mom that the president *did* come. I told her it wasn't on the news for security reasons. I told her I got to interview him (I was student government secretary or something), and I also told her that the secret service agents wore Hawaiian shirts so they wouldn't stand out or look conspicuous. I told her that I asked him about the O.J. Simpson trial and I described his suit in detail.

This was no white lie. My mom, in all her excitement, told the rest of my family, who told everyone else they came in contact with, and I spent the entire weekend a (lying) hometown hero. I'm sure lots of the adults were skeptical, but I just kept going into more and more detail about how great the president was and how it was a big secret, so that's why it looked like he wasn't actually there.

A week or so later, the doubts got the best of my mom (maybe the Hawaiian shirts tipped her off), and she went to my teacher for the truth. She didn't shame me, she didn't even tell my teacher about my crazy antics; she just found me in the kitchen, wrapped me in a massive hug, and whispered, "I know about the president." I confessed the whole thing and cried every single time I saw Bill Clinton on TV for years to come.

My mom knew something important, I think, that kept her from losing her mind on me for my crazy sinful lying. She knew that I wanted to be perceived as better than I was, and I think she knew that for most of us, that's the root of all our lies. We want to be seen as better than we are.

That was over twenty years ago, but I'm going to go first

and confess, friends—I'm still a liar. My lies have gotten smaller and more acceptable. Over time, I've gotten even better at it. Sometimes it's just me I'm lying to, sometimes it's the people I love the most. But the temptation remains for me to present a better picture of who I am to the world *constantly*, and I know that the consequences for honesty are seemingly too much for my fragile soul to bear. Let me dig in and give you some examples of lies that you might relate to:

Sorry you haven't gotten that already. It's in the mail!

I'll be praying for you!

So sorry I didn't see I missed that call.

I'll be there in a second.

If you do that one more time, you're going to your room.

Yes, we can't wait for our family reunion!

No, I'm not jealous!

So sorry, something came up!

I'm fine.

Ladies, I know that Christ has changed me and I'm not that wounded fifth-grader anymore. I know my identity in Christ is as a truth-speaker. And yet I'm still here, in this fallen world, often falling prey to the schemes of the Enemy who would have me believe I need to lie in order to be accepted. And I have a feeling you do too. So on this one, we lose as well. We're two for two on the list of things God hates, you and I. It's not looking good for us to come out of this thing unscathed.

HANDS THAT SHED INNOCENT BLOOD

Wait for it! For some of us, this might be where we can get off the train! I ran over a cat once (accidentally, don't get feisty with me) and I've killed about 3,045 roaches since I live in downtown Charleston, South Carolina, but do those really count? We could say I'm probably okay, right? Well, wrong.

> "You have heard that it was said to the people long ago, 'You shall not murder, and anyone who murders will be subject to judgment.' But I tell you that anyone who is angry with a brother or sister will be subject to judgment." (Matthew 5:21–22)

Well, shoot. If murder and anger are on the same sin shelf, I'm guilty here too. Maybe according to some layers of this description, I'm okay—but the truth is, I'm not. I know it, and I have a hunch that you're not okay either. While a large part of me feels tender and wants justice and peace for the innocent, I know at times there are murderously angry and vengeful feelings in my heart. I know that my scale of what is innocent and what is evil is incorrect. I know I've found another part of my heart that is worthy of God's anger, judgment, and hate.

LET'S DRAW A CIRCLE

I could keep going, friends, or we could stop here and throw our hands up. Thank God we've been girded with grace, wrapped tight in the breastplate of righteousness, or else we'd be falling all over ourselves in condemnation right now.

I haven't drummed up these verses and truths to leave us stranded, but I have brought them up intentionally, and I want to make a point that I hope we can leave on the table for the rest of this book, maybe for the rest of our lives.

When we talk about holiness, the only place to start is with ourselves.

I think we have the freedom and the liberty to talk about other people's issues, but I'm going to explicitly discourage the women of God from looking to the left or the right where this issue is concerned for a few important reasons.

First, we've got enough issues in our personal heart space to take up our time. This is a basic Matthew 7, plank/sawdust issue. Don't spend time looking at the little specks of sin and stuff that God hates in the lives of the people around you, when you *know* the full-blown logs of ick you're walking around with. Just don't do it. Deal with your own brokenness and leave it to Jesus to deal with the rest.

Second, humility is holy. I'm a big believer in focusing on doing the right thing more than obsessing over not doing the wrong thing. So if you need encouragement to deal with your own sin first, remember that humility is holy and Jesus was our greatest example of this. He never sinned, yet He willingly took the blame for our sin. Philippians 2 encourages us to be like Christ, consider others better than ourselves, take humility all the way—so let's take it too far.

Finally, I think that working on our own holiness and owning our own sin changes the world. We're going to dig into this for a large part of the rest of the book, but I'll cut to the chase and spell it out super clearly: sitting at home and seething over the sin of other people doesn't help anyone. It frustrates you, it doesn't show love to them, and I can't see how it draws you any closer to Jesus.

But! When we sit quietly, get humble, look at our own hearts and *repent*, change, shift, and head out into our day ready to live differently and allow the Lord to make small, daily transformations in our lives—the world gets changed. When we respond to the call of holiness by looking at our *own* lives, the world is changed and people are compelled to look to Him for answers about their holiness.

So I'm going to ask that we draw a circle, friends. A small one, right around our own hearts, lives, mouths, and actions. I'm drawing one around myself, and I'm asking that you draw one around yourself, too, and no one else. My prayer and hope is that every single word we read and every single thought and/or conviction that the Holy Spirit stirs up in us is applied to us alone, for the rest of this book and our conversation about holiness.

CAR WRECKS OF SIN

Now I know what you're thinking, because I'm thinking it too.

What about figurative car wrecks, you say? What about when you see a friend who is careening forward in unholy living, about to crash, about to hurt herself and others? Isn't it fair to scream, "YOU'RE ABOUT TO WRECK THE CAR"? I'm talking about what happens when we see friends stepping into infidelity, making decisions that are going to physically harm others, or the kind of sin that has consequences that are going to impact the world in a grievous way.

Whoosh, that's real. I've been the friend watching the figurative wreck unfold. I've watched my friend speed forward with a pulsating heart, scared to see what happens next. I've been there to see the spinning start, guessing the trajectory of the crash and what collateral damage will occur. I've been the first responder, I've seen the smoke of someone's life rise around them, and I've sat by forlorn and broken as they sobbed or silently stared in shock at the wreckage their actions caused.

I've also been the one to screw up my life with sin. Inside my head I can watch the playbacks of the years I spent hiding secret sin, pretending it wasn't eating away at my soul. I'll never forget the day I entered a college dorm bathroom intending to act on the eating disorder that had been boiling beneath the surface for months. I can picture myself just moments before I had the hard conversation with a friend, the one wherein I said words I can never unsay. I can see myself in the calm before the storm, in the moments when I was about to screw it up, and I wish someone had said, "You're headed for a car crash. This is going to be bad. Pull over."

Sin is no joke. It will mess up your life. And I get that when we talk about holiness, there is real tension that rises up in us. We need to have the freedom to call out to others who may be driving their car into incredible danger.

Here's what I've found, though: when we stay in our humble circles of personal reflection, weighted by humility and held tightly by grace, calling out to another who is in danger looks a lot more loving and a lot less judgy. And I think that for the most part, those cases are the exception and not the rule. The day in and day out things for which we find ourselves judging our brothers and sisters are not necessarily car wrecks waiting to happen. They're occasions where the daily, abundant grace of God breaks in and holds us together.

In *Wild and Free*, the book I coauthored with my friend Hayley Morgan, we talked about this concept of calling one another up and not out. We encouraged women to stop continually confronting one another with their sin in a way that speaks shame and condemnation, instead of grace and hope. We proposed a new way—the idea of calling each other up, continually showing each other how we're image bearers of God. This looks like a lot of encouragement and cheering one another on, but even in the hard conversations—even in the situations where we have to enter in with one another and talk about sin, we're calling each other up and not out. We're reminding the women of God who they are, instead of exposing them and leading them to believe they can be found unworthy of His grace.

So I think that even in the car crash moments, this is what it looks like: We get to live accountable toward our holiness first, we walk in humility about our own ever-present need for the good news of Jesus. Then when the time comes, if we have to, we shout lovingly, "It looks like you're headed for a crash!" Our friend is used to our voice speaking life and identity over us, so they trust us. This isn't another poke in the long line of our judgy rants. This is a shout from a sister, and the recipient feels spurred on and seen by us, and so—in most cases—if the Holy Spirit allows her, she hears the shout in love. And in the best-case scenario, she pulls over, and the horrible thing that was coming is avoided.

But you know what? Let's say she doesn't have ears to hear.

Let's say you did all the things right, but she still doesn't receive your gentle, humble, firm shout of warning. What does someone do who is broken first over their own sin, concerned with their own holiness, and humbled by their constant need for Jesus? I think they run to the site of the accident. And without saying, "I told you so," they give aid in whatever way God calls them to. I don't believe this means we try to fix the consequences of every person we know who runs off the rails in sin, but I do think it means we live like family. And family doesn't disappear after a big mistake.

CORPORATE FEELS

I'd love to set up another potential exception to this concept of staying inside our own holiness circles. I'm a lover of spiritual gifts tests. I like personality tests too, but give me a good spiritual gifts test or a ministry skills quiz and I'm all over it. I'll take it and have everyone else I know take it so we can talk about it. My favorite one is the Five Fold Giftings Test. There are many versions of this test, but I first became aware of it when reading the book *Building a Discipling Culture* by Mike Breen and Steve Cockram. Their version of the test is based on Ephesians 4 and it assumes that most of us have a base ministry gift, one of the five listed in Ephesians 4—apostle, prophet, pastor, evangelist, and teacher.

The reason I love this test so much is because every single time I take it, in any form, I get mostly the same response. I'm a prophet through and through. For the sake of this test, we're not talking see-the-future prophet or have-dreams-that-come-true prophet. We're talking about the gift of prophecy in a much broader sense.

Prophets are often able to stand back from circumstances to

get a clear picture of what is happening and therefore see creative solutions and develop a vision for situations others don't see. They understand the times and what people should do.* The way I've heard it described, prophets see the problem first, then they typically see the solution, and a lot of prophets learn that the best way to lead is to *be* the solution.

This makes the role of prophet sometimes hard to nail down, because if the situation calls for a pastor, the prophet might act as a pastor. If the state of a community is in dire need of a pumped-up, excited evangelist, we might see a prophet take on that role, even though that's not necessarily their strong suit. But mostly, the prophet feels the problem, and I'll tell you—I never feel like anything BUT a prophet.

If you and I went on a taco date and you were to talk for thirty minutes, I could probably tell you approximately three things I think you could do to fix whatever situation you're in. It's certainly not because I'm uber wise or delight in judging people; it's because my ears and my heart gravitate toward finding the problem and working on a solution. It's an occasional strength that can often turn into a weakness. I have to submit to the Lord and ask Him to sift, soften, and help me to love people well rather than discourage them. I cry a lot on election days, I can't watch sad movies or TV shows, and I can *always* find some kind of sin to confess because I'm a prophet. I perceive the problem first, and it usually takes some supernatural help from God for me to move on from it.

So what does a prophet do when she genuinely wants to be concerned with her own circle of holy ground and she doesn't want to spend her hours judging others? Or what do any of us do when

---

* See fivefoldsurvey.com.

we perceive the sin and brokenness around us? You're probably perceiving that most of our modern Christian community is blind to our holiness issue—what in the world do we do with that? How do we walk forward without yelling at everyone else about how messed up it all seems?

Here's how the prophets of the Bible did it: they walked through their message first. They received it first. I try and do this same thing, to a degree, when I teach publicly. I aim to get alone with the Lord within twenty-four hours of speaking, and I try to journal a little about how I need to respond to whatever truth I am about to bring to the people who will be listening. The prophets of the Bible did this too: they often took the hard truth God was speaking, walked through the discipline or correction themselves, then shared it with the people. They offered to go first and literally lived out the example of the obedience God was asking for all His people.

Hosea married an adulterous woman to live out the message God had for His people. Jeremiah went into captivity before He told God's people they'd go into captivity. Ezekiel—this one is weird—was made to lie on his side for 390 days to symbolize the judgment that was about to come upon his nation. The prophet often walks through the pain so he or she can have compassion when it's time to call the people to repent.

That's what I think we need to do here. I believe we have traded holiness for grace as individuals. I also believe we have traded holiness for grace as a church and as a community, and we need to find our way back to an abundant acceptance of both.

Is it a serious problem that we need to spend time in prayer over, that we need to ask God to heal? I'm going to say yes. Is the process of restoration for our generation going to come with us stepping up higher, elevating our voices, yelling at the masses and telling them that for goodness' sake, they need to remember who they are in Christ alone? Well, no.

If you've got the corporate feels, if you carry a prophetic burden for all of us to know God as He longs for us to know Him, the healing is His and the Holy Spirit is the main communicator. To partner with the Lord in restoration, we're going to have to step off the podiums and go ahead and fall to our knees. I think like the prophets of old, we're going to have to go first—repenting, returning, weeping, and setting our eyes back on Jesus.

With humble and secure hearts, we're going to have to draw a circle around ourselves and throw our hands in the air and say, "It's me. It's me. I'm the problem. I'm the one who does the things God hates. It's me who has forgotten how lavish and needed God's grace is. It's me who forgot the holy ground I was purchased to. I'm the one who got off course and somehow misplaced my purpose, my call to mission."

I think that if for the rest of this book, and really, for the majority of our lives, if we can keep our attention on dancing in the grace we so desperately need (rather than deciding who gets it and when), if we can stand firm in our identity as righteous daughters of God—bought with a price and placed in proximity with God (instead of measuring how everyone else is living), and if we can run fervently ahead with our eye on the prize of telling as many people as possible about Jesus, we can change the world.

But I think it starts with me, right here in this circle, the one who still does things God hates, the one who is needy, the one who is hopeful. I'll go first.

Let's Study the Word:

JONAH 4:1–4

But to Jonah this seemed very wrong, and he became angry. He prayed to the Lord, "Isn't this what I said, Lord, when I was still at home? That is what I tried to forestall by fleeing to Tarshish. I knew that you are a gracious and compassionate God, slow to anger and abounding in love, a God who relents from sending calamity. Now, Lord, take away my life, for it is better for me to die than to live." But the Lord replied, "Is it right for you to be angry?"

Oh man, if only I had room to insert the entire book of Jonah right here, I would. But you know what? You've totally got time to go read the whole thing. It'll take you about twelve minutes, so I'm going to encourage you to go do that. Read *The Message* version if Bible language trips you up. Just promise me you'll read it—even if you've heard the story a million times already and know all the Jonah elementary-school Bible songs. Are there songs about Jonah? There should be. What a goofy guy. Go read the whole thing and I'll meet you back here.

DON'T BE LIKE JONAH

We talked about prophets in this chapter, how they're entrusted with this weighty job of bringing truth, and how many of them had the interesting experience of processing the burden of their message before or in the midst of sharing it with the people they were called to minister to. But um, not so much with Jonah.

Basically, Jonah was entrusted with this beautiful message of repentance and grace. He was supposed to go tell the people of Nineveh, "God is holy, you're far from Him, repent or He's going to work out some justice in your life." Beautiful. Hard truth, but beautiful.

Instead of grace from the get-go or burden for the people, instead of applying the message to his own heart, Jonah immediately decided what God should hate: the people of Nineveh. Instead of aiding in the relief of their sin, he became complicit in it and chose pride (one of the things God hates), and ran from the Lord. For the record, I'm also a little surprised "straight-up trying to run away from God in a boat" isn't on the list of things God hates, but don't let me step outside my circle of holiness too much, right?

Jonah never sets foot inside his own circle of holiness; he is only continually peering at everyone else and judging what should be happening to them. I think it's extremely important to see what he ends up missing out on. Does God still use him? Yes. Does he still have a relationship with God? Yes. Do the people still hear truth and turn to the Lord? Yes. Does God still do His thing and stay consistent with His character and love people? Yes. Including Jonah? Yes.

So what does Jonah miss out on by focusing on the sin of others and never letting the eyes of his heart be opened to see his own issues? He misses out on joy. He doesn't get to experience the anticipation of a person running on mission, feeling the hope tinged all around the burden, the light just begging to break through. Even after God rescues him from the fish, he doesn't stop to count the fruit and dance all around about his life being spared.

When the miraculous eternal work of restoration and redemption happens in Nineveh, who should be the one with his hands held highest in the air? Whose heart should feel the lightest and the most full of praise? Who misses out on the most joy? Jonah. And let's not even start on the tree. Our boy J can't even stop to say thank you when God miraculously grows a tree to give him some shade as he is busy sulking like a six-year-old out in the hot sun.

Jonah doesn't just snub the grace God continually extends toward him, but he also resents the grace given to others. Talk about dancing in grace. Can you imagine the celebration in Ninevah? Jonah could have been leading them in a new line dance, but he's missing out because he just didn't want God to give them what they so desperately needed.

We don't just hurt the people in our lives when we choose pride over grace; ultimately *we* miss out. Everyone is going to bow and worship God one day—the Bible tells us so—and everyone is going to see that they need grace one day. The choice is ours to receive it now and dance in it, or sulk now and get it later anyhow.

The everlasting process of people being drawn to God, repenting, and telling other people about God is not going to stop until Jesus comes back to earth to restore the whole shebang for good. There is nothing we can do to prevent the kingdom of God advancing, and the rest of Scripture makes it clear that when we stay silent about Him, the rocks cry out and all of nature proclaims His glory and grace.

When we refuse to deal with our own sin and obsess over the shortcomings of others, when we accept grace as if it's no big deal and something we were owed anyhow, when we spend our days and our hours outside our own circle of holy introspection—we miss out. Grace still prevails. Conviction still comes. The Spirit of

God still does the work He's promised to do. Redemption presses on. The cycle of broken people being made whole keeps going. It's only our participation and our joy and our abundance that is up for grabs.

We've got a choice, women of God. We can talk about holiness while we're side-eyeing other people's circles, measuring everyone else against standards that we ourselves can't stand up to. Or we can continually take hard looks at our own actions and reactions, asking ourselves if we're living in a way that agrees with the holy positioning we've been given as daughters of God. We can do ministry in a way that cries, "Me too!" as we call people to the safety and peace we find when we're covered in the blood of Jesus. We can even speak hard truths and share His Word, but do it drenched in humility and aware of our own constant need for grace.

At the end of this story, we can be sitting alone and frustrated because God did what He said He would do, or we can be celebrating and dancing with the rest of our people, thrilled that we got to be a part of it. Let's not be like Jonah, amen?

Don't sit this one out. This dance is for you.

Let's Take It a Little Further

1. What would it look like to be more concerned with your own response to the holy ground we stand on as daughters than you are with the response of others?
2. Have there been times when you missed out on the joy of the redemptive work of God because you didn't want good things, grace, or forgiveness for others? How do you wish you'd handled that differently?
3. How can we logistically speak truth in love while not judging? What would that look like in your life, and how do you wish people would do that for you?

Chapter 4

WHY? AND REALLY?

THE TRUTH ABOUT HOLY
AND UNHOLY HABITS

Read by Kristen Beaumont

If we were together right now, I'd make a stupid joke. Maybe a slew of them, just to make you giggle and to shake out the tension before we ever get started. I'd probably make some kind of reference about us going into battle and needing to be prepared. I'd call out to you and say something like, "You got coffee, soldier? Have you taken your vitamins? Did you carb load? Okay, then we can proceed."

Because gals, we've got to go there. There's no way around it, only through it. So armed with grace, our circle of holy attention drawn around only us, a cup of coffee or tea, and maybe some pasta, we're going to take this mamma jamma of a minefield head on: I'm talking about alcohol. The sauce. Hooch. Liquid courage. Take your pick. I don't know how we could possibly wade through the water of current Christian culture talking about holiness without touching this massive landmine, even though it seems dangerous since we have so many different backgrounds and so many different viewpoints.

But I've always liked a challenge, so we're doing this. And I'll go first.

Here's my story with alcohol: As a young teenager, my first drink was out of a red Solo cup at a friend's basement party. It was your average American teenage situation—the parents were out of town, three people got invited, and three hundred showed up. Somebody's older brother bought a bunch of liquor, mixed it all together with some nasty old fruit juice, and it all went downhill from there. I don't remember much from that night, but I do remember feeling like I wanted to die the next morning. It was spring break, which fell during Holy Week, right before Easter. I kept my hangover hidden from my family for much of the following day, but twenty-four hours later I was still feeling incredibly ill, and I ended up tossing my cookies in the middle of our church's Maundy Thursday service, where we were observing the Passover in commemoration of Jesus's last human week on earth.

So—that's cute. I'll just let you hold on to that memory of me barfing my brains out somewhere between the matzo and the lamb.

For a few years, my relationship with alcohol continued like that. While maybe a lot of teenagers drink because of peer pressure, I always knew my drinking was about way more than fitting in. I craved the warm, emotional numbness that hit around my sixth sip, and that's what drove me back time and time again. As a teenager, my heart was so overwhelmed with FEELINGS, I loved the ability to not feel so deeply under the effects of alcohol—to be like all the seemingly carefree kids around me for a moment.

I had strong feelings about my worth and my body image— namely I felt worthless and disgusting, with my slightly curvier body and my rounder face. I felt left behind and confused almost constantly, because a lot of what held the attention of my peers didn't make sense to me. I never thought about college, I didn't care about sports, I didn't care about cars, I hated shopping, and extracurricular activities like newspaper, yearbook, and student government all seemed out of reach to me.

Halfway through high school, I gave my heart to Jesus and ran into the arms of some God-seeking friends. None of them drank or smoked or were sexually active, so I tried quickly to follow suit. By the time I hit college, things were different. The first Sunday of my freshman year, I attended a pretty conservative Baptist church where people mostly abstained from alcohol and never looked back. A few semesters into college, I went on staff with that church, and by my junior year, I was pretty sure I'd never touch alcohol again. I absorbed the beliefs of my culture and rejected the experiences of anyone else who might be able to consume it carefully and dare I say, worshipfully. I made a blanket decision that alcohol was *unholy*. You know, until I decided it wasn't again.

I quit the church job my last semester of college, mostly because I began to realize I'd filled every free moment of my collegiate years with ministry and work. I lived with my best friends, although I rarely spent time with them, and I was minutes away from getting married, settling down, and never tasting "free time" again. (Side note: Such a lie, right? Every season has free time.) So I quit the church job and spent a little more time with my roommates and my fiancé, and wouldn't you know? All of them had the capacity to have a glass of wine responsibly with dinner. I didn't like the taste of wine, but I quickly abandoned my staunch teetotaling position and tried to like the taste of it, or at least pretend I did.

Outside of an unfortunate bridal shower situation wherein I was emaciated and starving from a ludicrous pre-wedding diet, I never got drunk, and it was fine. I also never had more than one drink, and life didn't feel like it required a whole lot of numbing. I was getting married! We were young and had our lives ahead of us! I'd made it through college! It felt simple and pure to partake. And so I did.

At this point in the story, we're going to skip about six whole years ahead and I'll sum up what happened during that season in one sentence: I birthed and nursed four children in the span of seventy months. There was just zero time for alcohol. Who could drink when you had to be constantly downing water to keep your breastmilk supply up and coffee to stay awake? No relaxation for me! A glass of wine only kept me from the laundry pile, and there were no fancy dinner date nights for us in that season. Date nights looked like a salad snuck into the movie theater, but mostly we cheers-ed each other with coffee cups and bickered over whose turn it was to get the baby this time.

Until . . . church planting. In 2013, when our youngest baby was only six months old, we moved our family of six to Charleston to plant Gospel Community Church. This was our first solo church plant, my husband the only pastor, and the five of us were the only current attendees. Eventually some friends moved to join us, and our precious little team of ten began putting its hands to the work of the kingdom in our beloved town. We met our neighbors, settled into jobs and friendships, handed out fliers, and did a lot of praying. But you know what else we did? We learned a lot about the culture we'd moved into.

Downtown Charleston is a little bit like a mix between Disney World, an old movie, and Never-Never Land. It's *beautiful*—like incredibly beautiful, rich with history on every corner, and filled with people who love to play and enjoy life. They like boating on the weekend, beaching it up on weeknights, shopping on King Street, having picnics in the park, and they *love* their restaurants and bars. I don't want to paint a picture that's all play and no work, but it's a tourism hot spot for a reason, and interestingly, it's the consumeristic and playful lifestyle that's been the hardest for us to adjust to.

We didn't want to become like the people we were there to serve, but we did want to understand them, and we also wanted to be *near* them, so it felt important to enter into their rhythms in a godly and redeeming way. We adjusted our budget and schedule and made weekly date nights a thing. We also encouraged our people to dive into the weekend brunch culture. Everyone in Charleston eats brunch. Shoot, people drive from all over the country to eat brunch here. So how could we go about reaching our neighbors, understanding them, and pointing them to Jesus if we didn't first meet them at brunch? Like I said, they love their restaurants, so we went to the restaurants to meet them. And I started having a weekly drink. Just the one, on Thursday nights, as a celebration of making it through another harrowing week of church planting and as a nod to my newfound city.

One drink. Once a week. No problem, right?

Here's where I need to be honest that I'm fearful I could lose you for one of two reasons: (1) I think a lot of you might already be feeling a little judgy about the one drink. And with that, I'm going to lovingly and lightly tell you to get back in your circle, girlfriend. We're not talking about your holiness, we're talking about mine for a second, and (2) I think there's also probably a contingency of you who might want to discount what I'm about to say because I'm only talking about one drink when you've battled an issue with alcoholism, or walked with someone up close who has. And to that, I'd say—that's fair, but stick with me if you can.

The problem, and there was a problem, is that while I didn't have a drinking problem, I did have a drinking rhythm. I love rhythms. You can find them sprinkled throughout my entire life. On Sunday nights I answer emails, on Friday nights I fall asleep on the couch while "watching" a movie with Nick, on Thursday mornings I do a long run, I go grocery shopping on Tuesday, and every night before I conk out I watch about five minutes of *The West Wing* until I fall asleep and pick up where I left off again tomorrow.

My newfound drinking rhythm went something like this:

On Sunday we'd have church, and on Sunday night I'd feel so relieved that we'd made it through another week. On Monday, I felt overwhelmed by the mix of small business and small church ministry. On Tuesday I spent a ton of time in meetings and in community and wished I had just one day to act like the introvert that I am. On Wednesday I'd start looking forward to Thursday. On Thursday I'd spend all day looking forward to date night. Thursday at lunch, I'd start looking at restaurant menus online—picking out what food I'd eat and what drink I'd have. On Thursday afternoon I'd post a picture on Instagram talking about how much I was looking forward to date night. On Thursday night at about 8:08 p.m., I'd savor my one drink to the last drop, and on Friday morning I'd start looking forward to Thursday again.

I'd developed a pattern of work and relief that was no longer glorifying to God, even though from the outside it didn't look overtly sinful. I didn't get drunk or wasted, I rarely went past the first drink, and yet this controversial Christian issue was becoming a stumbling block for me.

WHY? AND REALLY?

The problem with my drinking was the why. It wasn't the when, the what, the how much, or the who with. The problem was the why.

It just helps me relax.

It signals my brain that we're now in the fun zone!

I deserve a little treat.

It's easier for me to open up and talk with my husband.

The troubles of the day just float away a little quicker.

Everyone needs to hit pause on the stress of the week, especially people in ministry!

Suddenly I'm back inside the confines of my sophomore-year soul, desperately looking to numb an overwhelmed mind because of a stressed-out schedule. I have confused something that is a blessing (the ability to be overwhelmed by the glory of God) with a mini-god that will bring me relief. My why is incredibly messed up, and my why has forgotten the power of Him who began a good work and will bring it to completion.

I can't pinpoint the turning point, when I started hearing the quiet pleas my heart was making through my drinking rhythm, but I will be vulnerable and tell you it didn't happen until I started writing this book. The problem with a rhythm that doesn't look dangerous from the outside is that it's hard to see the danger that lies just beneath the surface. I wonder if lots of us aren't walking around with rhythms backed up by why's that are missing the power, sovereignty, and goodness of God.

I started looking at my own "why" intently one day when I was reading about my absolute favorite (other than Jesus) man in the Bible, John the Baptist. Here's why I love John so much: he was basically a weirdo just like me. I have a feeling that if John grew up in America, he'd cock his head to the side and look just as blank as I did when people started talking about the football game coming up Friday or the student government elections. John was a man who had a sense of eternity and a sense of destiny—he knew the whole world was hurtling toward some immutable everlasting, and that's basically all he could think about all the time.

I also love JTB (that's what I call him for short), because he often felt the freedom to get real with Jesus, either by reverently worshipping his cousin the Savior (Matthew 3) or by questioning Him in love when things were looking rough (Luke 7). John was a man without a filter, on a mission, and about His Father's (and His cousin's) business. And he ate bugs, which is either super cute or terrifying, but definitely a little hipster, right? Now we call it foraging, veganism, and living green, but John was pulling those stunts when everyone else was eating lamb like it was going out of style.

So in Luke 1, we read the story of JTB's dad, Zechariah, being visited by an angel with the news that he and his wife, Elizabeth, (who was barren and older at the time), were going to have a son, John, who would end up being quite special.

Side note: In general, the book of Luke is my number-one favorite gospel, because it's written by a doctor who was sent by his boss to go check out all the hullabaloo with these new Christ followers. What follows is a fact-filled, beautiful, wild story about a Savior who lands on earth and turns everything upside down.

And because Luke was notorious for getting eyewitness testimony and then corroborating it with other sources, the details of his accounts always make me smile. Because this is a TRUE story, a historical account, and when we remember we're talking about real humans who lived and walked and slept and ate, it's all the more interesting.

This first chapter of Luke is no exception to this detailed storytelling, where we read about an incredible occasion. Zechariah is interrupted by the angel Gabriel on his most important day of work, only to find out that he and his old, barren wife are going to have a baby. Here's the best part: when he doesn't believe the angel, Gabriel causes him to GO MUTE until the baby is born. Can you imagine Elizabeth's pregnancy? I'll tell you this: not even once did she have to hear a side remark from her husband about how much her ankles were swelling, and that feels like a win, right?

Elizabeth does go into seclusion at this point. The Bible doesn't tell us why, but I think every woman who's ever lived through pregnancy would say: TO AVOID THE QUESTIONS. It's hard enough answering, "No! I'm sure it's not twins!" when you're only sixteen weeks pregnant with one baby—can you imagine being Elizabeth? Your man came out of the temple weird one day, can't talk, and now your belly is growing rapidly—even though she was estimated to be around eighty-eight when she gave birth to John. That's some weird stuff, so I'm pretty sure that even if I was THRILLED to be used by God and having a miracle baby, I'd be kicking it inside the house too.

There's also all this foreknowledge about JTB, his life and his ministry, and what he'll be like. And one of those fun facts that Gabriel lets Zechariah and Elizabeth in on? John the Baptist will abstain from alcohol and all fermented drink. We don't get much "why" behind this decision from sweet angel Gabe.

What we do know is that fermented drink was a normalized part of society in biblical times—for centuries it had been used medicinally, and it was oftentimes regarded as safer than drinking water, since water purification wasn't as easy as using a Brita back then. The Bible *is* clear about not abusing alcohol, not chasing or allowing intoxication, but for whatever reason, John isn't supposed to touch the stuff at all. Some scholars speculate that it's because he was promised to be filled with the Spirit from birth, and maybe it needed to be totally clear that he wasn't drunk. John was also in the line of Levites, the chosen line of Old Testament priests who were required not to touch alcohol. Some commentaries talk about John needing to be set apart from the rest of society. I'm sure we could all fill in the gap with our own ideas about why it seems helpful that John was going to abstain, but the fact remains—the angel of the Lord doesn't give us a clear why.

So one day, while I was thinking about my drinking rhythm, I got obsessed with John's "why," and I realized that the reason I was so fixated on finding his why was because I didn't feel solid and justified about *my* "why." I had fallen into a rhythm that quickly became autopilot, and anticipation of my one Thursday drink overshadowed my ability to anticipate God showing up in my week. I'm not proud of this, I'm not recommending this, but I'm telling you how it was.

My personal interpretation of Scripture and my experience have led me to believe that the consumption of alcohol can be God-glorifying. I see people do it all the time, without getting drunk, without sinning, because they enjoy the taste or because they're interested in the flavor and the history of the wine—shoot,

I even know some people who use it medicinally, just like in the Bible. But my reasoning for consuming my once-a-week drink didn't have anything to do with that.

I didn't trust God to provide rest, relaxation, rejuvenation, and joy, so I developed a rhythm that would enable me to get those things a different way. I knew the easiest way for me to relax was to numb myself, even with just one drink, and I was not actively believing that the power of God extended to my soul enough for me to find comfort in Him alone.

I began to pull the string of my "why," and I added on a new question that was equally offensive to—well, myself. After I asked myself why, I began to ask, "Really?"

Let me explain: If the answer to "Why have that drink once a week?" was "Because it helps me relax," then the follow-up question would be something like, "Really? Do you *really* not believe the Lord wants to help you find peace in the midst of your week?" Or maybe the next question would be, "Really? Do you *really* think peace and rest comes from two hours of not feeling things as deeply because you've had a strong drink?" Or even, "Really? Do you *really* not know that God has a plan for you to live in abundance that is so much greater than anything you can find in a restaurant or bar?"

Asking myself these questions hasn't been pretty, and it hasn't been fun, and it also hasn't meant that I've 100 percent cut any and all alcohol out of my life again. Let me describe what a new, normal healthy rhythm might look like for me in this new season of asking myself "Why?" and "Really?"

It all starts on Friday, seven whole days before the potential drink occurs. On Friday, I now work really hard to take a Sabbath. A few months ago, my husband and I repented about our lack of rest and started taking Fridays as our day of rest. It hasn't been tidy or immediate, but we're learning to be pretty fastidious about this day. We drop the kids off at school, and he goes to the beach to walk while I go to the gym (introverts unite), then we meet up around lunch time or visit with friends or take a nap—right there in the middle of the day. At three p.m. we pick up the kids from school, and I try to say, "WELCOME TO OUR SABBATH!" or something equally cheesy when I pull around the carpool line. That night, we eat food that is a small indulgence—either pizza or ice cream, or we have a fire in the fire pit and make s'mores. Something that says to our tummies and our souls, "We're not trying to get ahead here. We're resting. We're celebrating the week that is behind and the week that is ahead."

And how does the pizza and ice cream feel different from the Thursday night drink? Because it certainly could be just the same, a vice or a comfort in place of God's presence. However, it feels different on that Sabbath Friday because it's enjoyed in worship, not as a substitute for His fullness, but as a celebration of Him and all He's done in our week. When I've lived my whole week dependent on Him, taking full advantage of the access I have to Him, I'm not collapsing into Friday looking for a way to numb my heart. I'm dancing into the weekend, thanking Him for what He's done, even if it's been hard. For some people, I think it could be a glass of wine instead of a bowl of ice cream enjoyed in a holy way, but in our case it just isn't because come on with any chocolate/peanut butter ice cream concoction. I feel like that's how Jesus would celebrate the Sabbath if He was on earth today.

After the kids go to bed, Nick and I still watch a movie, and I still typically fall asleep about fifteen minutes in. But all the while, we're trying not to use our laptops or get stuck on business calls.

We're not holding any meetings, and we try to avoid social media. I don't do laundry or clean any toilets, and I try not to freak out when the kids leave their book bags right by the door like they're barn animals. We're Sabbathing. We're resting.

On Saturday we play with the kids, we catch up on laundry, we visit with friends. Nick takes the afternoon to work on his sermon, and I almost always work on Saturday nights. I try to make sure the house is semi-picked-up for Sunday morning and check to be sure that there's food in the fridge for lunch and dinner. Sunday mornings start early-early. Nick does sermon prep, and I take care of the kids and then lead our pre-service prayer time at church. By the time we tear down our mobile church and eat lunch, it's usually three p.m. The whole house goes dark for about two hours while we crash, then we go on a family walk and eat a meager dinner. When the kids go to bed on Sunday night, Nick and I go over our plans for the week, syncing our schedules and encouraging one another to take pockets of rest and take things off our plates.

On Mondays I drop the kids off at school and drive straight to the beach. I feel like God has asked me to fight the fast-paced-fear-based feeling of Monday with prayer and praise, so I do that by walking on the beach. The rest of the day is meetings, meetings, meetings, school pick-up, karate, gymnastics, then church meetings at night. Tuesday through Thursday looks a lot like Monday, with a balance of work, family, and ministry, except now I'm scheduling pockets of time for sanity. There are scheduled blocks for exercise, reading the Bible, and showering. I plan them like I plan the rest of my week, and I try to keep to my schedule as much as possible, not so that I can have a tidy life but so that I don't collapse near the end of the week in exhaustion.

So now, when Thursday night comes, I have a choice. Do I want a glass of alcohol because of the taste, because of the experience it adds to my meal? Or am I just as happy without it? Many nights I find I'm just as happy without it—but the point is that I'm no longer crashing and burning into a crutch to find my rest and my comfort. I asked myself "Why?" and then I asked myself, "Really?" and what I found is that God is enough for me. He's enough for me on the rough days, He's enough for me when my plans fall through, and He's enough of a treat when I know that I've been working hard at what He's called me to all week long.

The plan isn't foolproof, and there are moments where I need a massive dose of grace, where I have to try again, or where I realize that I was lying to myself about my why. And there are other crutches, replacements for God I have to watch out for and which you might too: exercise, Netflix, gossip, food, shopping, Instagram, and even reading are a few of my other go-to numbing devices, so I keep watch over my heart concerning those as well.

And here's the thing: maybe none of these relate to you. Maybe your issues are totally separate, and numbing isn't even your problem. However true that might be, I'm willing to bet there are areas of your life that have become so normal and routine, you may have forgotten what they mean to you. And to that, holy woman of God, daughter of the Most High King—I'm daring you to ask yourself "Why?" and "Really?" I believe the Holy Spirit living inside you will give you a far truer answer than I ever could. I believe He'll reveal things no one else can see, and I think you'll find that abundance is on the other side of obedience when it comes to asking those questions.

LET'S DO THIS TOGETHER

I'm inviting you into a holy experiment with me, right here and right now. We're going to look at our hours, days, and weeks together and ask a few questions. I want you to know that I'm asking myself these questions because this is an evolving tension we walk in. I can't believe that once I rooted out the dependence on my Thursday drink, my predilection to find comfort in this world would never come back, can I? This is a series of questions we get to continually ask ourselves as women who are safe to acknowledge our sin, as women who know that the fullness of joy is found in Christ alone. So let's dive into the next few questions together, with zero shame, and with open eyes to see any crutches we're leaning on more than the comfort we find in Christ alone.

First, do you see any rhythms, habits, or indulgences in your life that might be quietly replacing Jesus? Here are some to look for, but I highly suggest getting still and quiet and letting the Holy Spirit speak louder than my suggestions: calling your sister or best friend, exercising, eating, watching TV, using Pinterest, scrolling through social media, working on the budget, making a to-do list, drinking coffee, spending lots of time alone, binging on being with people, or even reading. These are not dangerous things, but these are not the source of our life, are they?

What is the Lord stirring in your spirit? Are there any convictions or confessions you need to talk to Him about? Any patterns you already see, or are there some that you didn't even notice until you slowed down to take stock? Remember: we dance in grace, and it compels us to change. No room for shame here as we move on to the next question in our group experience.

Our second question is this: Why do you engage in this activity? If you're not sure, here's a good place to start. How do you feel prior to seeking comfort from something in the world, and what do you believe it will accomplish for you? For some of our examples, this might be clear. I *feel* discouraged, and when I have alcohol, I don't feel those things for a few hours, and that's why I drink it. I feel tired, but when I drink a lot of coffee, I have temporary energy. I was angry at my husband, so I called my sister, and she helped me process my feelings. I feel insecure about my body, but after I spend an hour exercising, I feel like I'm more in control. I feel overwhelmed about all that's on my to-do list, so I take a few minutes to surf social media and tune out my life. I feel scared about the future, so I spend some time making a to-do list and organizing my calendar, just to be sure I know where I'm headed.

Again, we might not find dangerous-looking things when we search our hours to see where we seek comfort. But it comes down to *why* we're doing them and what we believe the response will be. Will it be temporary or permanent relief that we find? Will what we're doing meet our needs or will it exacerbate the issues we already have?

Finally, let's ask ourselves, "Really?" Do we *really* believe that God is who He says He is and will do what He says He'll do, and if so, should we be spending our days running after these worldly comforts?

If we really believe Isaiah 9:6, which tells us Jesus is the Prince of Peace, why would we believe we can find peace in a plan, schedule, or budget? Yes, those things are helpful tools. But they're most helpful when we've gone to God for peace first, and we plan as an act of worship. When 2 Corinthians 1:3 tells us that God is the God of all compassion and comfort, does it really make sense to seek the advice or encouragement of a friend before we run to Him? He might use the friend to minister to us, absolutely, but can't we trust His ability to soothe our hearts more effectively than any other?

We could go on and on and on, and I would encourage you to stretch this experiment all the way out in your own life. What things are you filling your hours with, why are you doing them, and what are you hoping to gain? Do you really believe God is enough and better than anything this world might offer to give you what you need? Are you approaching activities *with* the Lord, having already taken full advantage of what He has to offer, enjoying His blessings as worship? Or have you begun to worship the gifts—forgetting that they're not what your soul truly craves?

HOLY OBEDIENCE AND ABUNDANT FRUIT

I think that asking "Why?" and "Really?" is so important because there's more for us on this earth than subsistent living—filling up on what culture offers us as good. I mean that with all of my heart. John's "why" for abstaining from alcohol was simple obedience, and that was enough for him. When we look at all that Jesus offered him in return, that "why" starts to make a lot of sense. In Luke 7:28, Jesus calls John the Baptist the best man who was ever born. I don't think it was only familial pride that made Jesus boast in John, and I don't think it was the fact that John didn't drink. I think Jesus loved John, delighted in his purpose, and fulfilled it with vigor.

My friend, my beautiful friend, if you are in Christ, do you know that God has a BIG, GOOD, GOD-GLORIFYING, ABUNDANT plan for your life? Do you know that it's not selfish, it's just truth, to repeat the fact that Jesus died so that you might have the freedom to step into that abundance, whatever it is in particular for you? The most quoted passage about abundant life is John 10:10 and goodness gracious, it's one of my favorites:

> "The thief comes only to steal and kill and destroy. I came that they may have life and have it abundantly." (ESV)

The root word for "abundantly" here is *perissos*, meaning "exceedingly more, going past the expected limit." The word for "life" is *zoe*, and it encompasses our physical presence and future eternal existence.

Jesus came so that we would have a physical presence and future eternal existence that is exceedingly more than we might anticipate, going past the expected limit. Amen, amen, amen, am I right?

Well here's the deal: the world's definition of "more" and "abundant" is not God's vision for more and abundant. If abundance is exceedingly more, going past the expected limit of life, we've got to check our hearts to be sure we're not just expecting God to produce exceedingly more, going past the expected limit of *stuff*. It's the age-old struggle: **Do we want more of what God can give us, or do we want more of God?**

Let's say we're already past that struggle, which I believe most of us have probably settled in our hearts. We want God. We love the blessings He gives us, we love the people He's given us to walk with, we're trying to love the work that we're doing for His glory. But if you pressed us, we'd say it's Him. It's always Him. It's relationship with Him that we desire the most, and it's nearness to Him that satisfies our souls.

I'm going to talk in human words about holy things right now, so I'm praying for grace and for truth to permeate where we're about to go.

Romans 8 says nothing can separate you from the love of God; not death, life, angels, demons, nothing you've done in your past, present, future, not any power, not any height, depth, NOTHING can keep us from the love of God. James 4 says if you draw near to God, He will draw near to you. Isaiah 65 says when we call, He will answer. Jeremiah 31 says He draws us in with loving-kindness. Jeremiah 33 says if we call, He'll answer us and show us great and mighty things. John 15 says if we abide in Him, He'll abide (remain) right back in us. Ephesians 3 says we have unsearchable riches in Christ.

We are always the variable in the equation of our intimacy with God; His willingness to give all of Himself has never been up for debate, if by grace and through faith we seek Him.

If you are a woman wanting more of God, there is nothing on earth that can cut you off from the fullness of God and His love for you. What's more, there is no one who can tell you that your behavior, or anything else for that matter, can separate you from Him. There is nothing YOU can do to cut yourself off from His steady stream of life either. You are given all access to Him all the time.

Backtracking to make sure we're all on the same page: We're daughters of God who want only God. We're daughters of God who can get as much of God as we want. Thus, we can get all that we want—in fact, we have all that we want in that we have all of God. But the crazy important question is: Why don't we feel it? Why don't we *feel* like we live in abundance, even if that more/ abundance we're longing for is more of God?

I believe it relates to our honest questions of "Why?" and "Really?" We don't *feel* like we live in abundance because we are taking our needs to the temporary, less-than-perfect comforts of this world that always leave us empty and wanting more. Simply put, we don't live in abundance because we choose the world over abundance. I believe that our actions and our decisions are either agreeing with our proclamation of only wanting God (and having Him!) or they're agreeing with an untruth: a belief that this world *does* have something to offer us and a desire to find our needs met outside of the Lord alone.

When I step into my weekly drinking rhythm looking for peace, solace, comfort, or release, am I agreeing with the truth that the love of God is all I need? Am I acting in accordance with the truth that God is enough? When I zone out on Netflix, with what truth am I agreeing? When I use words that dishonor God to say things that break His heart, am I agreeing that I'm a citizen of heaven whose needs are met? When I use my body to fulfill my flesh sinfully, either through lust or overeating or over-exercising—to placate my soul and attempt to find my place in this world, am I agreeing with abundance? Am I agreeing with what God has spoken over my life?

The real question, at the heart of our actions, is this: Who do we believe? Do we believe in the world's definition of abundance or God's?

I believe that once we've danced in grace and drawn a holy circle of God's righteousness around us, we can have a more nuanced and mature conversation about holiness. We can move past whether things are seemingly right or wrong, good or bad, and we can begin seeing what is at stake. Women of God: whether you're looking at your own lives or the lives of other people around you, the question isn't whether someone is living right or backsliding or screwing around or messing their lives up. The question is: Are we agreeing with the abundance that God has spoken over our lives or not? Are we acknowledging that we have absolutely everything we could ever ask for in Jesus, or are we believing there is more on earth for us to enjoy besides the riches of Christ that have been made ours as co-heirs of His kingdom?

As we look at the patterns of our lives, the ones that might be sinful, the ones that might be gray-areas, the ones that might seem neutral or mundane, this is the question we've got to ask ourselves: Do we believe we're standing on holy ground or not? Do we believe the abundance of God is ours right where we're at? And if so, how in the world does that shift how we live? I believe that armed with that truth, we'll make more decisions that mirror the abundance of God. We'll make more God-inspired moves that look like we believe Jesus is all we need. We won't be driven by fear, shame, or a desire to become holy—because in the name of God, we already are! And when we make a misstep, when we ultimately sin (since we're still subject to this fallen world), we'll get right back up, dust off our clothes, dance in His grace, and stand firm once again.

John didn't drink, and that was what abundance looked like for him. The Holy Spirit is a better instructor than I'll ever be, and I believe He'll give you insight and wisdom into what abundance looks like for you. I pray He'll be loud and clear, and that He'll give you the boldness to ask yourself "Why?" and "Really?" with a smile on your face and hope in your heart. I believe that in Christ, you're already holy, right where you stand, and I believe you'll receive exceedingly more of Him throughout your life as you continue to make decisions that agree with the abundance you have in Him.

Let's Study the Word:

JOHN 3:22–30

Listen, if you think the Bible isn't full of spicy stories about people getting drunk, you're totally wrong. Noah gets a little weird in Genesis 9 and leaves his robe open while he's sleeping off a rager. Alcohol leads Lot to do some terrible and horrible things in Genesis 19. Isaac mistakenly blesses the wrong person in Genesis 27 after he's been drinking (and eating). Basically all of Genesis after the garden reads like an embarrassing family history.

Nabal, Ammon, and Uriah are all characters from 1 and 2 Samuel who have lessons for us to hear about how things go wrong when we've had too much wine. Psalms and Proverbs have dozens of verses for us to read through. It goes on and on, and we could dig into this issue, but I think for the good of our hearts and the sake of His glory, let's stick with John the Baptist for a little longer, and get even closer to the heart of the issue.

After this, Jesus and his disciples went out into the Judean countryside, where he spent some time with them, and baptized. Now John also was baptizing at Aenon near Salim, because there was plenty of water, and people were coming and being baptized. (This was before John was put in prison.) An argument developed between some of John's disciples and a certain Jew over the matter of ceremonial washing. They came to John and said to him, "Rabbi, that man who was with you on the other side of the Jordan—the one you testified about—look, he is baptizing, and everyone is going to him."

To this John replied, "A person can receive only what is given them from heaven. You yourselves can testify that I said, 'I am not the Messiah but am sent ahead of him.' The bride belongs to the bridegroom. The friend who attends the bridegroom waits and listens for him, and is full of joy when he hears the bridegroom's voice. That joy is mine, and it is now complete. *He must become greater; I must become less.*" (emphasis added)

We know that alcohol was off the table from the beginning with John, and even though we're not exactly sure why, we do see some conditional rewards—this consecrated life he lived worked for him; it was in his favor, and God blessed him for it. Well, take that and rewind it—*was* John blessed?

I mean, sure, he's a well-known guy in the Bible. He had a large following of disciples. He got to baptize Jesus. Jesus even said John was his number-one fave guy, so that's cool. But he also lived a life of ridicule and misunderstanding. He always played second fiddle to his younger cousin, Jesus. He was jailed and then eventually beheaded for living out the ministry that he never got any praise for in the first place.

I'm playing devil's advocate because of course, I believe John was super blessed. I think we're still talking about him today because he honored the Lord so well and served Him with such vigor. I think he's probably one happy little hipster in heaven, worshipping for eternity and wearing all kinds of crowns. I'd imagine that every crown Jesus gave him, he gave right back, and he's right where he wants to be: joyfully giving praise and glory to the one true God, the rescuer of his soul.

The thing about JTB, and holiness, and drinking—what all

of this stirs up in us is this: What's our prize? What is our aim? What is our goal here?

The reason why I think the above passage of Scripture has everything to do with drunkenness and holiness is because I believe that glory in ministry might have been one of John's biggest temptations. I don't know what your biggest temptation is, but I know that mine is basically changing day by day and month by month. I know that on Thursday nights, the biggest temptation for me is to tune out, turn off, and numb the sensitive awareness that God has given me for a reason. When I'm confronted with the possibility of abusing alcohol or eating too many cookies or watching too much Netflix, the temptation is to stop believing Jesus is enough for me.

So in this story, I see John the Baptist confronted with some grumpy disciples who are basically saying, "Why are so many more people going to get baptized by Jesus? Aren't you the guy? Aren't you special? Who *is* He?" These guys are messing with what is potentially one of John's biggest temptations, and we're about to learn from how he reacts.

John responds, telling them, "'I am not the Messiah but am sent ahead of him.' The bride belongs to the bridegroom. The friend who attends the bridegroom waits and listens for him, and is full of joy when he hears the bridegroom's voice. That joy is mine, and it is now complete. *He must become greater; I must become less.*'" The actual prize for John is not the glory he receives from doing the work of the ministry, but following Jesus. The minister who started it all, he makes his declaration so loud and so clear (John 3:28–30). Jesus IS enough. Jesus IS the prize. He is the ultimate "why." The joy IS mine when I serve him—when I'm out here in the river, when I'm in jail for the sake of His name, or when my head is literally on the chopping block. It's Him that I want, it's Him that I've got, and *I am blessed*.

When I read this passage, I believe God might be inviting us to the heart of the issue. John is telling us that Jesus is not the cherry on top of a life of ministry for him; Jesus is the ultimate why behind everything he does. John is showing us *Jesus is the prize*.

I believe God might be inviting us even deeper into the holy place we've been purchased to, to explore the ground where we've been placed as daughters of God. It seems as if so many women of God in this generation aren't even aware of the positioning they have in the kingdom—they don't know they're on holy ground, they haven't been told they don't have to work to get there. No one has unloaded the truth for them that the way they live has the potential to agree with their holy identity. Instead they falsely believe that their actions determine their standing with God.

We get to pray and hope and actively seek to tell the believers among us, "Look down! You're already on holy ground! You've already been saved. And His saving work means something; you'll experience more abundance when you walk in obedience and peace—when you dive in deep to the nearness that comes with abiding in Jesus, not the pleasure of this world!" Not only do we get to tell them all of that, but I think we also get to invite them to take a second look at that holy ground and see they've got all the prize they'll ever need *in Him*.

Whatever is tempting us to believe that something other than Jesus will bring us joy, peace, completion, satisfaction, or happiness, John the Baptist is here to remind us that the joy is ours in Jesus. No matter what hardships are behind us, we're still blessed. He is enough, and He is the prize.

Let's Take It a Little Further

1. Is the Lord piercing your heart, bringing to mind an issue where you've stopped asking yourself "Why?" and "Really"? Share it with someone, and most of all, share it with Him. Acts 3:19 says that repentance brings refreshment, so no matter how big or how little it seems, tell someone.

2. What's your prize? When you evaluate your days and the things you hold dear, is Jesus the prize? If you believe it with your mind, what would it look like to believe it with your actions?

3. What's your trigger issue? As you look at your life, do you see any misplaced dependencies? Any habits, hopes, patterns that might be taking the place of your hope in Jesus?

Chapter 5

TEACH US HOW TO PRAY

WHAT HAPPENS WHEN HOLY WOMEN TALK TO A HOLY GOD

Read by Ann Swindell

We called ourselves the Good Girls Gang. Katie, Molly, Emily, Courtney, Lauren, and me. We found each other at a new youth group during my junior year of high school, and we were inseparable. If this sounds cheesy and silly, it is—but man, it was a sweet and beautiful season in my life.

I'd gone from partying with red Solo cups and making out with boys in the backseat of old cars to riding around town sober with these girls, dancing to Beyoncé and attending Bible study together. I started to believe that maybe being a Christian wouldn't always be lonely and sad and weird; maybe it could be fun, and maybe I could still have friends.

We had each other's backs, the Good Girls Gang and me. We spent our days, nights, and weekends together, and we occasionally got into super deep conversations about the Lord, which I loved. And for spring break? We were going on a mission trip together. I couldn't wait.

So we packed our bags, and with full hearts headed to Nashville. Y'all, I'm going to give it to you straight—I don't know that we did any actual mission work. Maybe the real mission was to keep a bunch of Christian kids out of trouble over spring break, and if so, I wholeheartedly support that objective. It worked. The trip was fun, and it forever changed my life. I remember eating tacos and seeing Music Row. I remember that we recorded a hilarious song together in our youth pastor's dad's recording studio. I remember seeing a beautiful college campus, and I remember overdramatically crying a little because everyone climbed a tree and I didn't exactly have the athletic prowess to join them.

One night, the Good Girls Gang stayed up freakishly late—I mean like four a.m. or something stupid, and in between doing little pranks and dares in the bonus room of our host's home, we met God in a new and beautiful way.

It started with simply talking *about* God, talking about prayer, talking about what it really looks like to follow after God—and then we started asking each other some honest four a.m. questions. I remember someone asking why we closed our eyes when we prayed. Next, we started evaluating why it seemed like our voices changed when we talked to God—why did we use different words, sweeter tones, more formal gestures? As we sat scattered around the room, hunched in our sleeping bags, deliriously sleepy, we asked each other, "Do we believe God is here right now?" Do we seriously believe He is present? And if we do, how does that change how we live?

We were essentially asking this: Is God really our friend? And if so, can we access Him just like we do one another? I think we were also flexing our "why" muscle by identifying characteristics of our prayer life that weren't necessarily honoring to God, but were more about impressing other people.

In the midst of this pretty-in-depth-for-a-bunch-of-high-school-gals conversation, we embarked on a late-night spiritual experiment. We started praying out loud and just kind of redirected our conversation with one another while allowing the Lord to be a part of it. As we addressed one another, with our eyes open and our voices casual, we'd also address the Lord. It looked something like this:

MOLLY: (who was actively moving, using the elliptical machine that was in this spare room, but looking at us girls) I want to know the Lord more intimately. I want to know what it's like to be actual friends with Him. (with her eyes still open, voice unchanging) Lord, I want to know You better. You've called us Your friends for a reason; can we act like it?

COURTNEY: (addressing us as she lay on her back, staring at the ceiling) Man, me too. Can you imagine what it was like to be a disciple of Jesus? That must have been crazy to see what He was doing up close. God, will You help us do that now? Will You work in our hearts and give us eyes to see You, even when we don't see You?

JESS: (sprawled out on the air mattress, with one eye open and hands clutching my stomach) I love you guys. I'm so glad we're talking to each other and Him like this. It feels life changing. But here's the thing: we've stayed up too late and now I'm starving. Lord, I'm heading to the kitchen. Please help me to not wake up the boys in the other room, and please let there be some Oreos available.

As silly as it might have seemed, I think we all unlocked some newfound belief about our potential intimacy with God that night.

We stopped seeing Him as far off and far away. We stopped seeing Him as untouchable and unreachable. We started believing all that the Bible says about the space that's been purchased for us in the throne room of God, and we went there. We acted like we were daughters of God. We acted like He was our friend.

I've carried the memory of that night with me for sixteen years, because I experienced some gentle but meaningful breakthrough—even though I was so fresh in my faith. For the first time, I started talking to God like He was my friend, like He was in the room, like He was listening. And I knew, without a doubt, that He was.

A RESPONSE TO THE INVITATION

Therefore, since we have a great high priest who has ascended into heaven, Jesus the Son of God, let us hold firmly to the faith we profess. For we do not have a high priest who is unable to empathize with our weaknesses, but we have one who has been tempted in every way, just as we are—yet he did not sin. Let us then approach God's throne of grace with confidence, so that we may receive mercy and find grace to help us in our time of need. (Hebrews 4:14–16)

If I found a simple boldness in my faith that night in Nashville, I'll be honest and tell you that my childlike communication with God didn't stay uncomplicated forever. Over the years, I've seen the simplicity and friendship in my conversation with Him slip away and come back again, finding myself often vacillating wildly between two different responses to the access I have to

God through prayer. Sometimes I'm walking boldly into the throne room of God with my words, and other times I find myself struggling to take His invitation to intimacy seriously. Oftentimes, I've let doubt, complacency, or even an assumption of my own spiritual maturity (and therefore, lack of neediness) keep me away from conversation with God.

A few years ago, God began to remind me of that night in Nashville, of how I'd seen Him as an uncomplicated, albeit holy and complex, friend that I could talk to. I began to share this idea of unhindered interactions with Him while traveling to write and teach.

In *Wild and Free,* I wrote about my daughter, Glory, how she comes down the stairs in the morning already in conversation. Literally, as each foot finds its place on the wooden steps leading to our family room, her words are already coming and they're directed at one person: her dad. She talks as she walks, she keeps talking as she curls up in his lap, and eventually when she does stop talking (usually after detailing her plans for the day and what she'd like to do), her eyes rest gently on his face, waiting for him to respond. It's this picture that daily reminds me and compels me to the feet of Jesus. It's this privilege that's been purchased for me that keeps me coming back to Him. Just to talk. Just to tell Him what's on my mind. Just to wait and see how He'll respond.

What I've found as I've shared these thoughts is that the women of God respond to this message in varying ways. I've noticed that some women seem to find this concept of unfiltered communication with the Lord almost novel—it's refreshing, and it equips them in ways they haven't been before. So many women seem to say, "Oh man! I forgot about just talking to God. I've made it too complicated and forgotten that I have such open access to Him."

But there's also the other response. I've found that some

women reject this message of simple communication with God as too elementary, like information they already know, and they're ready to move on. Depending on what day you catch me, I can completely resonate with either camp. Some days I'm all, "PRAYER IS THE BEST. I JUST TALKED TO GOD IN THE CAR." And other days I'm rolling my eyes at my husband when he suggests that I ask God about a question I have.

I can tell that a lot of us might vacillate between these two responses because I've watched the women of God respond, some letting their mouths drop gently open, remembering the days and years that have passed by wherein they haven't taken advantage of the nearness to God that is theirs through Christ Jesus. And I've watched other women quietly and knowingly shut down, discounting this truth as too simple or elementary for their taste, ready to move on to more in-depth study.

I think one thing that could be keeping us from stepping into the freedom of talking to God as our holy birthright is our confusion regarding grace and holiness. Perhaps sometimes we're not grasping the depth of depravity and separation sin causes, so we're not realizing the incredible free gift we've been given through intimacy with God. Prayer seems commonplace, stuffy, maybe even contrived. Then maybe there are seasons where we *get* grace and feel the sort of freedom that has broken us from the chains of what time with God "should" look like. We're not slaves to ninety-minute quiet times, and we may not be memorizing whole books of Scripture, because we understand grace and the fact that walking with God isn't about how much we can produce or how much shinier we can get.

But in the quest to grab and spread grace, specifically as it pertains to how we commune with God, an important truth has been trodden over:

We don't have to communicate with God because it makes us more holy; we *get* to communicate with God, and our ability to do so is a miraculous gift from Him. We don't have to pray; we *get* to pray.

Yes, we are free from the false belief that the amount of time we spend with God equates to the growing level of our holiness. We're daughters of God who currently stand on holy ground, not because of our merit or our works, but because of *His* work in our lives and the sacrifice of Jesus on the cross. We're not required to put in hours of spirit-work, repeating rote phrases and empty words, memorizing and decorating the outside of our souls with religious trophies of knowledge. *We still get to talk to God.*

We don't get to talk to God because it's good for us or because it's the wise thing to do. We get to commune with God because it makes us feel better. We get to commune with God because it's in Him and through Him that we find our home. We get to talk to our dad because He wants to talk to us, because He loved us first, and it's a privilege and an honor and a huge gift for us.

And on the other side? Sometimes it might feel juvenile to us, like it's something we should have already learned. We may wonder if we shouldn't be throwing around bigger words and ideas, doing a little heavier lifting as women of God. We might feel like we should have graduated from simple prayers and moved into more complex "quiet times." This is the God of the universe we're talking about here! Doesn't He demand more attention? More focus? Shouldn't we hold Him in such high regard that we treat Him with reverence? It seems to us in those seasons that we shouldn't be throwing around such casual words, and maybe we could use a little less talking about how we feel and a little more theological study.

Goodness gracious, I've been there. I've wanted to call women to deeper places with God, because I've longed to go there myself. I've longed for structure in my prayer time, concerned that if I don't have a plan or a method of talking to the Lord, I'll just ramble or make it all about me. I've thought that if it was as simple as just communicating with God, then everyone would do it, and we'd all be more spiritually mature—so surely walking in relationship with God can't be that simple.

While we're representing all groups, I've got one more on whose behalf I'd like to communicate. I've experienced this myself and heard from a number of women that sometimes simple communication with God doesn't work for them for a variety of reasons. If you find yourself in this camp, maybe you've tried to explain to others that you don't feel anything when you talk to God or that, conversely, you feel too much. Perhaps you've had a bad interaction with your father and it makes relating to God as a dad hard for you. Goodness gracious, that's real. I hear that.

Maybe some of you feel too pragmatic and logical to talk out loud to an unseen something. Maybe you were made to pray often as a kid, and it seems too traditional or carries connotations of disingenuous religious patterns. Perhaps prayer was used as punishment in your life or it was forced on you in a way that left you believing it's something we *should* do, not something we *get* to do.

Wherever you're at, I want to sit with you for a second and just say, *it's real.* It's all real! Those feelings are real, and you're allowed to feel them. But now, we're going to speak truth to them so that we can move on and grow.

If you've believed (truthfully!) that grace covers you and you don't *have* to pray, I want to say, amen! You don't have to. But in Jesus's name, you get to. Psalm 84:10 says that one day in the house of God is better than a thousand anywhere else. That's some truth we can stand on, and the simplest way I can reiterate it is this: talking to God is better than talking to your sister, watching Netflix, drinking coffee, exercising, chocolate, sex, reading fiction, searching on Pinterest, or doing your makeup. It just is. Not because it's good for you like going to the doctor is good for you. It's good for you because your soul is hidden in Christ and most at home with the Spirit of God working on your behalf as you communicate with God your Father.

Prayer is better for you than all those things because our God is the author of peace, comfort, love, truth, beauty, joy, abundance, grace, mercy, and *life*. Talking to God, just being in communication with Him, is where heaven invades earth and we experience a little of eternity in the midst of our everyday. And the craziest part? Because we're walking suits of the Spirit, image bearers of an unseen God moving and living here on earth, we can talk to God while we do all those things! However, I still think it's beneficial for us to have moments set aside wherein He gets our undivided attention, because why wouldn't we want the love of God, unfiltered and uninterrupted? If you could have one-on-one time with your best friend, you'd take that over a quick catch-up while you're doing your makeup, right?

The argument that you might not have time to spend with God is just a little silly, because you have your entire day. Talk to Him while you're driving your kids around. Talk to Him while you're in the shower or using the bathroom. Get chatty with the King of Kings while you're walking the dog or doing the dishes, and cry out to your Father while you're putting on your blush or sorting through the mail. This is our holy and divine right as daughters of God, and it is not something we have to do; it's what we get to do. It's enjoyable. It's fun. It's literally life giving.

For the holy women of God among you who would like us to

move on from talking about prayer in such an elementary way, I'm going to have to beg you to read the words of Jesus from Matthew 18. I particularly love *The Message* version:

> For an answer Jesus called over a child, whom he stood in the middle of the room, and said, "I'm telling you, once and for all, that unless you return to square one and start over like children, you're not even going to get a look at the kingdom, let alone get in. Whoever becomes simple and elemental again, like this child, will rank high in God's kingdom. What's more, when you receive the childlike on my account, it's the same as receiving me. But if you give them a hard time, bullying or taking advantage of their simple trust, you'll soon wish you hadn't. You'd be better off dropped in the middle of the lake with a millstone around your neck. Doom to the world for giving these God-believing children a hard time! Hard times are inevitable, but you don't have to make it worse—and it's doomsday to you if you do." (Matthew 18:2–7)

He says it so clearly—it's *better* for us to receive and return to childlike, simple faith. I don't think that means that we neglect growing, learning, and maturing spiritually—but I think it means we fully ingest the truth that we'll always have to come back to these elemental tenets of walking with Jesus. I think that for as long as we're alive, we'll need reminders to be in communion with God. What's more, I think that the fruit we'll produce while simply abiding in Him will always be deep, never shallow.

I find concepts of theology in Scripture—building blocks we can shape our beliefs around—and I see where we get wisdom about weighty concepts like God's sovereignty, predestination, sanctification, and more. But I do not ever, ever hear Jesus telling His followers to grow up and move on from the simple obedience and abundance that comes from walking closely with Him, day in and day out. The truth is, I don't think spending time with God is all that simplistic or basic to begin with. I think that when the women of God walk boldly to the throne with confidence, hoping to receive mercy and grace and truth and Jesus—well, that is some graduate-level Christianity right there. That's the real deal. It shifts you when you spend time with God; it shifts the way you live and love others.

Last, for my friends who have lost faith in the accessibility of God or the benefit of seeking His face, I would just encourage you with a simple idea that might shift things for you. Prepare your hearts and have a pen ready.

TRY IT. YOU'LL LIKE IT.

I know it doesn't *feel* simple. I know you have preconceived notions about what will happen. I understand that it might seem crazy to walk around the block and talk out loud to someone you can't see. It seems totally fair that you might have negative feelings about prayer, God as a Father, and the act of humbling yourself. But sweet friends, I'm begging you to try it. Not so you'll be better, not so you'll be a tidier Christian, not so we'll all be on the same page. I'm begging you to try prayer, to stretch the limits of your relationship with Jesus, because I believe you will be happier. I think you'll feel more at peace. I believe you will experience more of the spiritual fruit that has already been purchased for you, simply by placing your faith in an unseen relationship and acting on it.

My friends, whatever camp you're in, I'm saying that to dance, stand, and run in our beautiful faith looks like prayer. It looks like talking to God with the expectation that He hears us. And I don't think we *should* do it, I think we *get* to do it. So let's.

THERMOSTATS, NOT THERMOMETERS

At our church I'm in charge of the pre-service prayer time, and I couldn't be more grateful. We're into discipleship and raising up new leaders to replace us all the time, but friends, I super selfishly always want to be the one who is in charge of prayer on Sunday mornings because it's my absolute favorite.

If you ask what time church starts, we'll tell you that worship starts at 10:30, but really—*really*—we start at 9:30 because that's when prayer starts. A few years ago my husband implemented this little pre-service session and asked us to be thermostats, not thermometers. He said anyone can be a thermometer! Anyone can walk into a room and take the temperature of that room. Of course, the church has a spiritual temperature to take. Does it feel worshipful in here? Does it feel light or heavy? Are people communing with one another? Are they engaged or sleepy? Is today's rain making the day feel a little more laid back, or is the slight, rare breeze encouraging us to have some wild and spicy worship? Depending on the day, the people attending, the weather, the season, and a million other little factors, the church has a temperature, and we can either read it or set it. Our prayer time helps us set it.

I start prayer the same way almost every Sunday. I gather everyone around, ask Nick to give us a one-minute preview of his sermon, ask everyone to stand up (the temperature gets wonky when we all sit down), and then I ask our people, "Why do we pray?" I ask this question every week so that we can remind ourselves before we get started, so we can encourage anyone who has never prayed with us before, and mostly so we can just pause and remember that it's holy stuff we're doing—walking into the throne room of grace with boldness together. Here's what they say back to me each week:

We pray to set the temperature.

We pray because we can.

We pray because it bonds us together.

We pray because we need God to show up today.

We pray because He's listening.

We pray because there are people getting ready to come here this morning for the first time and we want to love them well.

We pray because ministry is hard and we need help.

We pray because we want the Spirit to move.

We pray because this is our revival, not a recital.

Their responses vary from week to week, but I always look each person in the eye, nod when they speak, and almost always follow up by saying, "Yes," "Amen," or "in Jesus's name." Once they've all had a turn to speak, they know what I'm going to say next. I officially kick off prayer time with my favorite thought about prayer: "We pray each Sunday morning because our people are on their way in here, and we want them to walk into the throne room of God. We want them to worship Him, to commune with Him, to experience Him. We pray to stretch out the space between earth and heaven, to clear the path between us and God, and to prepare a place for them where interacting with Him feels natural and normal. We pray to set the temperature. Now let's get after it."

That's why we pray on Sunday mornings, my wild church family and me, but why do *we* pray, women of God? Other than the fact that we get to? What does it do for us? How does it leave us changed? I'm glad you asked.

We pray to remember who He is

Recently I was on a trip to speak to a group of women about the Lord. I'd brought a friend along with me to be my companion. We got up early, met at the airport, talked about the weekend. After the flight, we grabbed some lunch, caught up on all our usual subjects, then checked into our room at the retreat center. As we were making our way down to the main room where the event would be held, three women grabbed us and identified themselves as the prayer team. They asked if they could pray for us, pulled out some anointing oil, and immediately began fervently praying over both of us, our time with the women of the church, our friendship, and our relationships with Jesus.

We walked away with gentle smiles on our faces, and once they were out of earshot, we expressed the exact same thing: We'd forgotten we were there at the retreat for the Lord to work in our lives. We'd forgotten He was going to move. We'd forgotten who He was for a minute, and we needed the gentle reminder of prayer to wake us up to the reality that He was about to do what He does best: move in human hearts, heal, bring comfort, and grow us.

We pray to remember who God is. We pray because even though we might know about Him and His Word, it's easy to forget about His character. We need the simple reminder that we have a God who has made allowance for us in His throne room, that He loves us, He cares for us, He wants us to be in relationship with Him. We pray because it impresses upon our souls that God is good, loving, big, and still altogether caring and intimate with us.

We pray to remember who we are

Just like we need the reminder that God is good and caring, we also need the reminder that we are His children. Prayer reorients our hearts to His and redefines the inextricable bond we have with our Father. When we take the leap of faith to talk to someone we can't see, when we ask Him for what we need because He's the provider, when we tell Him how good He is, we're not just talking, we're declaring our dependence on Him. He knows we're His kids and we know in our heads that we're His kids, but we often need to be reminded of that. We're not here alone, stranded and on the hook to produce a good life or make it all happen. We're the daughters of God. He's already fought all the battles we face, declared Christ in us victorious, and has sent the Holy Spirit to shepherd us through this life—while we bring everyone with us that we can.

We pray to remember where we are

I was talking with some good friends a few weeks ago about body image and all the pressure we're under as women. About half of the group proposed that we should absolutely fight against the expectations our culture puts on us as females—to be perfectly toned, plucked, tanned, and poised—but a few members of the group were feeling the pressure to belong more than they wanted to fight. One friend in particular said, "I hear you guys. I agree with you! But we live in America! We have to live here, under these constraints."

We all sat quietly thinking about that, mulling it over, feeling the tension with her. But ultimately God stirred up some conviction in my heart and I blurted out, "We don't live in America. We live in the kingdom."

We pray to remind ourselves what culture has rule over our hearts and what actual constraints and boundaries we're under. We pray to remind ourselves where we live and where we belong. We don't live in America or the UK or Australia. We don't live in Canada or South Africa or Germany. We, the women of God, live with our feet firmly planted in the kingdom of God, and frequent prayer reminds us of our citizenship. Prayer waves the banner of belonging over our hearts and lives, declaring, "I'm a kingdom girl! I'm not a slave to sin or a foreigner living in a world where I'm trying to fit in. I belong in heaven, but I've been sent to earth by God to believe and receive the gospel, and to be an ambassador of light, calling others out of darkness and into relationship with my King. I'm a kingdom girl."

We pray because somehow, miraculously, it moves God to work on our behalf

When I've heard teaching on prayer in the past, it's almost always centered on how it's good for *our* hearts. And I couldn't agree more, as you can see from the above points. But! But! But!

We can't ignore the fact that in God's Word, there are countless times when the people of God cry out to Him in prayer, His heart is moved, and He acts on their behalf.

One theological definition of God's character is that He's immutable—He cannot be changed. He can't be inconsistent with His own character, and He can't act not-like-God. Because He is not human or fallible, He can't be fickle or waver back and forth. Here's how Numbers 23:19 describes it:

> God is not man, that he should lie, or a son of man, that he should change his mind. Has he said, and will he not do it? Or has he spoken, and will he not fulfill it? (ESV)

But somehow, miraculously and mysteriously, there is some tension here for us to grasp. God keeps His immutable character, not changing who He is or His very nature, but He often does change the course of what is going to happen contingent upon the prayers of His people. God's all-knowing nature would tell us that even He knew He'd change the course of history, so it wasn't a surprise to Him, but there's no denying He does delight in switching things up as a direct result of prayer. Here are just a few examples:

When the people of Ninevah repent and pray, God saves them. (Jonah 3)

When Elijah prays for the widow's dead son, he comes back to life. (1 Kings 17)

When Moses prays for the Israelites and God doesn't kill them. (Exodus 32)

Jesus Himself tells us in John 14 to ask for things in His name and they'll be done! It seems simple and clear in the Word of God that we can ask God to do stuff, so why is it not so simple and clear in our hearts? Because many of us have asked and been disappointed. We've prayed for healing, for things we were certain we needed. We've prayed for the health of loved ones, for peace in Syria, for safety on trips where someone was hurt anyhow. We've prayed for strength and still felt weak. We've prayed for guidance, felt certain we received it, and then found that we'd made a mistake. We've prayed and asked God for help, and it has seemed like for whatever reason, His inclination or ability to answer our prayers is not real. Not only do we doubt in our own hearts, but many of us find ourselves hesitant to encourage others to pray, lest they experience the same letdown.

I could give you a party line here about how God is answering prayer even when He's saying no. I could remind you that we have no idea what God is up to, so He could be answering our prayers even when it seems like He's being quiet. I could tell you about my friend Jackie, who said she was able to praise God for keeping her son safe, even after he died, because wasn't He safe in Jesus's arms? I could give a simple answer about why we should keep asking God to move, even when it seems like He doesn't.

But I just don't think this is a simple-answer situation. God is very large, very wild, and He does what He wants. He's also very good, very dependable, and—I believe—always working things out for our good because He loves us. I think that prayer is a mystery, an act that changes us, but that we can undoubtedly believe it also changes the outcome of what happens on earth. I think that if we could figure it out or draw a diagram of how it works, it wouldn't be so holy or sacred. And if the hand of God could be charted and described in a few short paragraphs, He'd be more like a human and less like a majestic and worship-worthy ruler of the universe.

Prayer shifts us, reminds us of who we are and who He is. Prayer guides us to truth, giving us eyes to see where we live and why we're here. But when we look at the Word of God, we can absolutely stand firm on the truth that prayer often changes the outcome of what happens in our world. So let's be holy women of God who dance in the grace and mystery of a kingdom we can't quite grasp, and take our place as we talk to our Father.

Let's Study the Word:
JOHN 21:7–23

Then the disciple whom Jesus loved said to Peter, "It is the Lord!" As soon as Simon Peter heard him say, "It is the Lord," he wrapped his outer garment around him (for he had taken it off) and jumped into the water. The other disciples followed in the boat, towing the net full of fish, for they were not far from shore, about a hundred yards. When they landed, they saw a fire of burning coals there with fish on it, and some bread.

Jesus said to them, "Bring some of the fish you have just caught." So Simon Peter climbed back into the boat and dragged the net ashore. It was full of large fish . . . but even with so many the net was not torn. Jesus said to them, "Come and have breakfast." None of the disciples dared ask him, "Who are you?" They knew it was the Lord. Jesus came, took the bread and gave it to them, and did the same with the fish. This was now the third time Jesus appeared to his disciples after he was raised from the dead.

When they had finished eating, Jesus said to Simon Peter, "Simon son of John, do you love me more than these?"

"Yes, Lord," he said, "you know that I love you."

Jesus said, "Feed my lambs." Again Jesus said, "Simon son of John, do you love me?"

He answered, "Yes, Lord, you know that I love you."

Jesus said, "Take care of my sheep." The third time he said to him, "Simon son of John, do you love me?"

Peter was hurt because Jesus asked him the third time, "Do you love me?"

He said, "Lord, you know all things; you know that I love you."

Jesus said, "Feed my sheep. Very truly I tell you, when you were younger you dressed yourself and went where you wanted; but when you are old you will stretch out your hands, and someone else will dress you and lead you where you do not want to go." Jesus said this to indicate the kind of death by which Peter would glorify God. Then he said to him, "Follow me!"

Peter turned and saw that the disciple whom Jesus loved was following them. (This was the one who had leaned back against Jesus at the supper and had said, "Lord, who is going to betray you?") When Peter saw him, he asked, "Lord, what about him?"

Jesus answered, "If I want him to remain alive until I return, what is that to you? You must follow me." Because of this, the rumor spread among the believers that this disciple would not die. But Jesus did not say that he would

not die; he only said, "If I want him to remain alive until I
return, what is that to you?"

Every time I write one of these study sections, I almost start by
telling you, THIS IS MY FAVORITE PASSAGE OF SCRIPTURE.
I've held back a few times, but I guess that's one of the fun parts
about writing a book—getting to take women you love on a little
scrapbook adventure of your favorite parts of God's Word. So I'm
tempted to say it again here, because goodness gracious, I love
this passage so much.

Can I help you read it with a little more humanity smattered
into it right now? Jesus spent a few years hanging out with this
wild brood of disciples and getting to know them and all their
quirks. They went through a horribly trying, discouraging, holy,
and traumatic period together in the week leading up to Jesus's
death. Then He died and all the false hopes they'd placed on Him
to be some kind of enigmatic, revolutionary political leader were
dashed. They hid in a room, scared to go out and be seen because
people knew they'd been with Him. They'd missed all the little
signs and clues He'd given them about coming back, and let's be
honest—no one was expecting Him to rise from the dead.

But then HE DID. The women found out first, told the
disciples, who didn't believe them, and then Jesus Himself came
to see them, showed them the holes in His hands, and they were
all thrilled and excited, and they probably had all the feels. All
of them.

But then? Y'all, I'm going to give it to you straight. I'm not
sure what happens next. This whole thing is uncharted territory
because Jesus is fully man, fully God, has died, and is now living
in a resurrected body. He can seemingly walk through walls and

poof in and out of places. So one minute he's talking to them in John 21, and then next minute—poof! He's gone again. And what do those disciples do? They go fishing.

So that's where we find these precious little holy hooligans. They know Jesus is risen—thank God they've stopped hiding in the room behind the locked door—but they've gone right back to exactly what they were doing when Jesus first called them into ministry. They're fishing. And we're about to see how disciples interact with God once they've caught a little more vision of who He is.

I'M LOOKING AT YOU, JOHN

My sister is the oldest of six grandchildren born to my maternal grandmother and grandfather, and she has a nickname for herself that has made us giggle for the last few years, mainly because it's true. She started calling herself "#1" in high school, and was usually pretty quick to assert that not only was she the firstborn grandkid, she was also the favorite. I remember, when I was a teenager, basically wanting to kick her in the shins each time she said it, but it became hilarious when my Nana began to confirm it. In the last few years of her life, my Nana—who was the world's actual sweetest and most loving woman—got honest and lucid and basically hilarious. One of the things she was quick to tell us? Yeah, Katie was her favorite. Once Katie even recorded it on an iPhone video and sent it to all the cousins.

You'd think it would frustrate us or make us feel jealous, but because we love our Nana so much and because we love our Katie so much (Listen, she can't help it. She's everyone's favorite—including mine.), we ended up just smiling anytime we talk about it. You gotta love an honest Nana, and you gotta love a firstborn who knows her place.

John is basically telling us all here: "I'm #1." Earlier in John chapter 13, when he's retelling the story of the Last Supper, he's quick to call himself "the one Jesus loved" *and* let us know that he was basically nestled up beside Jesus while everyone else was just sitting around like normal. And here, even after the resurrection, he's doing the same thing. It's him telling the story; he knows people will know he's the one who wrote it, but he's still just making sure everyone knows, "I'm the one Jesus loves! I'm #1!"

I don't think John was Jesus's favorite, but I think that when a disciple grasps how deep and wide and high the Father's love is for them, they're forever marked and they feel like surely they're #1. It changes you, to grasp the depth of what He will do to be in relationship with you. It shifts you, to see the might and power and glory of the triune God and then to be served by Him, like a friend. I'm not saying we should all walk around claiming to be Jesus's favorite, but I think we can learn from the passion with which John believed God loved Him. Jesus didn't just say it, He showed it, and once John experienced that up close, there was no convincing him that he was just one of the crowd to the King of Kings and the Lord of Lords.

As we pray, women of God, I cannot fathom what would happen if we approached God with the certainty that He loves us, and if we walked into mission with the conviction that we are a top priority to Him.

This is for every one of you who has been told you're not that important or that you shouldn't bother God with the small details of your life. This is for every one of you women who is convinced you're #2 or #3 or #12 in your family. Jesus died for *you* that you might inherit the glorious riches of His marvelous light *and* walk in the truth that you're an ambassador, sent to tell others He loves them just as much.

I think what we can learn from John is that while we don't want to treat Jesus too casually, like He's just another guy, we can treat Him with familiarity. We can lean up against Him. We can declare and rest in His love for us. We can stand firm on the assumption that we're the one Jesus loves.

HE CANNOT STAY IN THE BOAT

For those of you keeping track, this is the second time (that we know of) that Peter willingly jumps out of a boat pretty hastily to get to Jesus (Matthew 14 is the other time). I've already told you how much I love JTB, but I also relate strongly to Peter. He is always saying exactly what's on his mind (hey, no filter), sticking his foot in his mouth, getting all violent and rowdy, and then falling all over himself to try and walk with Jesus. I'd say that's the last fifteen years of my life summed up as well, so yeah—I feel you Peter.

I am so blessed that Peter has lost all chill when it comes to Jesus. While John is so assured of God's love for him, Peter is so assured of something else: he wants to be near this guy, right now. In the past few weeks? Maybe not as much. There was the moment right before Jesus died when Peter denied Him; he let his fear take over and fell right into the Enemy's trap for his life. But right now? He just wants to be as close as he can be to Jesus, even if it means getting a little soggy.

Can we please lose all chill when it comes to Jesus? I'm

asking seriously. Can we take every ounce of self-respect, caution, propriety, self-preservation, and sophistication that we so long to be defined by and trash it? When a disciple has seen their friend serve, love, lead, perform miracles, predict His own death, die for the good of the whole world, and be raised again so that we can be raised to eternal life with Him, I think it's time to lose our cool a little.

Women of God, in our prayer and in our intimacy with God, it's time to get a little undignified. I'm okay with your quiet worship, hymns, and folded hands, if that is what intimacy with God looks like for you. But I fear that many of us are so concerned about the world's perception of us that we miss out on walking in the abundant, vibrant, wild, beautiful intimacy of a life with Jesus, lived out for the world to see. The problem is not that God is waiting for us to finally show Him we really love Him; the problem is that we may get to the finish line and realize we were playing it cool for no reason at all, other than our pride.

As we seek the face of God, let's go full out. Let's be like Peter—wet clothes and all. Because we have seen Him do the miraculous in our lives, and we know the full truth of who He is and what He came to do for us.

LET'S BE READY TO HEAR BACK

I can't handle the last few paragraphs of this passage. Sweet Jesus gives the nod to kooky, wild Peter and asks him to come for a walk. Can you picture Him standing up from the fire where they're gathered around eating fish, brushing off His robe with His nail-scarred hands, and gently flicking His head backward as

He beckons Peter to come chat with Him? I once heard a pastor speculate about that conversation, and he said many theologians think Jesus was giving Peter a heads-up about the fact that he'd be crucified for the sake of the gospel. I don't know what they were talking about in their private chat, but I do believe it points us to a dynamic and compelling component of being in a relationship with Jesus: his ability to respond.

From person to person and community to community, we're going to encounter various theologies and beliefs about the power of the Holy Spirit and the ways God continues to communicate with His people. It doesn't matter if you're in a community that believes in the practice of prophecy or if that kind of thing totally freaks you out; I think we can all agree that we serve a God who *hears and responds.* Somehow, in some way, God is not only able to perceive what we're saying, but He uses a variety of means to respond to us—His Word, the power of the Spirit in our hearts, and even other people.

Let's be women who interact with Jesus like His disciples did—silly excited, having lost all of our chill, and trashing our desire to be seen as dignified or respectable. Let's enter into conversation, not speaking into the air or reciting religious poetry into nothingness. Let's talk to a God we believe hears, cares, and responds to the people He loves so much.

It's His grace that paid our way here to this holy ground of confident familiarity and affectionate friendship with Jesus. We won't let that grace be in vain, but we'll soak it up and stomp our feet and enjoy the conversation, amen?

Let's Take It a Little Further

1. How would your life look different if you believed that you're the one Jesus loves? Get specific. What has kept you from believing this truth that is woven throughout Scripture?
2. How much is dignity a factor in your willingness to worship God freely? What would jumping out of the boat to get to Jesus look like in your life?
3. When was the last time you talked to Him? When was the last time you heard a response? These two things are intimately linked.

Chapter 6

DON'T TRY TO LEARN ME

WHAT HAPPENS WHEN HOLY WOMEN READ GOD'S HOLY WORD

Read by Rach Kincaid

My daughter, Glory, is what you might call a firecracker. Glo-bear (as I affectionately call her) hasn't ever faded or shrank back a day in her life. She comes into the room with a desire to impact it, she rarely doubts herself, and she pretty much feels the freedom to say whatever she wants—which is sometimes awesome and sometimes embarrassing. I could tell you serious stories about how God seems to have a miraculous hand on her life and has spared her physically many times. I could tell you funny stories, like the time I found her destroying political campaign yard signs promoting a candidate she didn't agree with (we made her fix them and apologize). And then there are stories like this one in which Glory is at her sassiest.

My mom had taken the kids one Saturday afternoon so Nick

and I could get some quality time together. Because she's awesome like that.

If my kids are with me for a Saturday afternoon, my main goal is keep them alive and maybe do some laundry. When my mom has them, they go to plantations or museums, make crafts and bake cookies, or do some kind of hands-on science experiment. I've decided I no longer have time to compare myself to my mom and feel insecure, so instead I just thank God that she's so stinking high capacity and that she's mine.

This particular Saturday afternoon, my mom and stepdad had taken the kids to some sort of historical site, and my three boys were eating up all the information. They're all three history buffs, thanks to their grandparents, and they were loving all the new wisdom and insight they were gaining about their home state. Mom told me later that Glory seemed a little less than enthusiastic; she was dragging her feet and scowling, arms crossed and eyes rolling at each new historical gem that was offered to her.

Apparently, after a few more minutes of this, my mom asked Glory what was going on and why she seemed so upset. Glory unfolded her arms, put her hands on her hips, cocked her head to the side, and said, "Listen. It's Saturday. Don't try to learn me."

Real talk: how many of us have felt this way? I wonder if you've ever walked through a season where you looked around and said, "Hey, hey! Don't try to learn me." Whether you're the type of gal who is always seeking more knowledge or not, I think in our hearts, there's often a small resistance to being taught. Let's see if we can fight that resistance together from where we stand on holy ground.

THE TALE OF THREE LEARNERS

There have been three specific seasons wherein I've become the kind of girl who is desperate to learn, and in particular, the kind of girl who is eager to learn about God. I feel my experiences reflect some of the ways I see other women approaching the idea of ongoing spiritual learning. I'm going to describe these seasons, but in reverse chronological order of when they happened to me.

I try hard not to walk in offense because I'm crucified with Christ and it's no longer just Jess here. It's Christ in Jess defending me, it's Christ in Jess changing me, and it's Christ in Jess forming my identity. But you want to know one of my stumbling blocks? It's talk that implies there is a rank-based system of spiritual depth, the subtle questioning of whether or not someone's faith or ministry is big-girl-Christian stuff or just baby-Christian stuff. I react when people talk about the supposed differences between people who seek out the "real meat" or "substance" of faith and the "spiritual snackers." This kind of talk rubs against my pride, bringing out all kinds of defensive and sinful feelings, and it's hard for me to let go. I find myself wanting to defend my faith and the ways I interact with God. I find myself wanting to campaign for a more pure, less haughty faith for all the women of God. I find myself wanting to feel offended, and then after that, I find myself wanting to prove people wrong.

Over the past year I found myself moving into a season of deeper study and more intense pursuit of spiritual learning. I cracked open some more archaic theology books and started studying Greek and Hebrew. I tried to share less "light and fluffy" thoughts on Instagram and chided myself when something I said was simplistic or elementary. I spent hours digging through books other people deemed worthy, but I confess the motivation behind the pursuit wasn't pure. All my learning was driven by fear, by the worry that someone would find out I wasn't wise, and by the desire to be seen as something more than I am.

After this season of reading a lot of books by dead theologians, a lot of podcast-searching and library visiting, my husband disarmed me with a casual question, posed gently. He walked into the living room where I was studying one day, with a sweet smile on his face as he pointed to one of my crazy thick books and said, "What are you doing, Jess? Why are you reading those books?" He continued to encourage me, saying that if I was reading them for some added knowledge, that was great—but if I was reading them to pretend I'm someone I'm not, then I should stop. I confessed to him how insecure and fearful I'd felt recently, writing a book about holiness when I believe I could easily be accused of having a simple, elementary faith. He reminded me, with so much love and grace, that God didn't ask those dead guys I was studying to write this book—He asked me. He reminded me that all I needed to know about holiness I could find in God's Word, and that the Holy Spirit is the ultimate decision maker when it comes to whether or not something is "deep enough."

I closed the big books and opened my Bible instead. I asked God for help and went back to writing with an intense conviction: this is the resistance that so many women of God must fight. I hadn't wanted to learn more about God for His glory, I'd wanted to learn more about God for *my* glory. I didn't want to fully receive the story of redemption that the Bible has to offer; I wanted to sit on top of it and appear to others as though I could recite it. I didn't want to use God's Word as a spiritual weapon to fight darkness; I wanted to use it as a shield in order not to be found lacking. I was learning, but I was not *growing*. I was seeking but not finding freedom. This, I believe, is an issue for a lot of us.

Some years previously, there was a season wherein I "drank the Kool-Aid" of a community and became branded more by the cultural constraints of that group than I was by the love and grace of Jesus. It was 2008, and I'll protect names and cities, but my husband and I moved to be part of a church we believed was shifting the face of modern Christendom. This growing young megachurch was led by a bold, dynamic leader who was comfortable making strong, sweeping statements. And *we* were comfortable following in the wake of his opinions, which could occasionally cause collateral damage. My extended family watched from the outside, and I remember them making gracious inquiries, prodding gently at our headstrong beliefs. My mom would say things like, "It seems like you're saying you think believers should only read this one version of the Bible. Is that right?" We'd reply, pridefully, with a strong statement—one we'd learned from the church we were attending. (FYI, I no longer believe that there's only one acceptable version of the Bible.)

Oftentimes, we didn't even wait to be asked our opinions—we'd seek out opportunities to show the newfound ideologies we were suddenly clinging to with such vigor. If you'd met 2008–2010 Jess, she would have told you exactly what the Bible and theologians had to say about predestination, women in the church, high-fructose corn syrup, yoga, celebrating Santa, and what ministry should look like. There is zero part of me that feels happy about the kind of haughty junk that came out of my mouth during those years. I can't think of many things in life I truly regret, but the way I treated other believers (even just inside my heart) during the years of 2008–2010 ranks high on my list.

There were beautiful things about that church and redeeming parts of our community there, but in general, we were a people eager to learn, eager to absorb knowledge, and quick to disseminate all the information we acquired. When Nick and I take an honest look back at what caused us to enter into that kind of learning environment, one of the characteristics that stands out to me most was our desire to belong.

I wouldn't call that church a cult, but that kind of climate is what draws cult members in, right? There's something comforting about knowing that you are IN. Grade school girls show us this by example. When you've got three little girls who all know the same secret about something else, you've got a pretty tightly knit community. Until there is a new secret, a new truth, a new community to form and be committed to. Watching the power plays of a little girls' sleepover can leave you feeling like you're watching the kind of political strategy planning you'd see in the White House situation room, amen? That's because little girls innately recognize that the secret to belonging is all in what you know.

Friends, the current church culture in our world isn't too different, is it? What we know and how we share it is continually and constantly the deciding factor when it comes to the question of community. We identify ourselves with the information we receive. Think about the way we identify with the books we read, the authors and speakers we follow, the podcasts we listen to, and the shows we watch. *This* is how we relate to one another. *This* is how we know where we belong.

Nick, my husband, is a reader for the sake of learning alone. He doesn't get caught up in following certain authors or pastors too much, and I've watched him disengage from conversations pretty quickly when they turn even slightly toward celebrity worship of different authors or leaders. I witnessed a hilarious exchange between him and another man the other day wherein the other guy kept asking Nick over and over who he reads. He kept saying, "I mean are you into Rob Bell? Spurgeon? Furtick? Sproul? Stanley?" Nick's heard of all those guys, but he knew that more than anything, the guy was trying to figure out which Christian culture camp he belongs to. Nick kept shrugging his shoulders and saying, "I don't know. I haven't read anything other than the Bible for a while." I don't think that poor guy who was questioning him ever got what he was looking for.

The early church leaders dealt with this issue, so we can be assured it's nothing new that we're suddenly struggling with. Almost as soon as Jesus left the earth, His followers were already taking sides and identifying with different groups and sects. They wanted to find their identities in groups defined by which leaders they followed and which new teachings resonated with them, even though the wisdom was always from God and the real teacher was always the Holy Spirit.

As long as you grab for what makes you feel good or makes you look important, are you really much different than a babe at the breast, content only when everything's going your way? When one of you says, "I'm on Paul's side," and another says, "I'm for Apollos," aren't you being totally infantile? Who do you think Paul is, anyway? Or Apollos, for that matter? Servants, both of us—servants who waited on you as you gradually learned to entrust your lives to our mutual Master. We each carried out our servant assignment. I planted the

seed, Apollos watered the plants, but God made you grow.
It's not the one who plants or the one who waters who is at
the center of this process but God, who makes things grow.
(1 Corinthians 3:2–7 MSG)

I find that a lot of women are learning and seeking wisdom
in order to belong more than they are seeking to simply know
God. Simply put, I think a lot of us are reading the Bible, reading
certain books, and listening to certain voices just to fit in. It's
not that we're not gleaning some goodness in there, but if we're
honest, it's not our first or foremost objective. Growing closer to
God is a nice by-product of all the learning we're doing, but it's
not the driving force behind these pursuits.

What's problematic for those of us who struggle with this is
that the baseline of what we "should" know is constantly changing
and evolving. It's not that the truth of God is changing, but the
voices who teach us are, as well as the ways we learn and the
subjects we're supposed to be learning about. It's almost like
defining your level of health with only the current information
available about how to eat healthy, which is impossible! In the
sixties, doctors told us it was okay to smoke and drink powdered
drinks. In the eighties, we heard that high-carbohydrate diets were
the way to go. The 2000s said no to carbs and yes to diet soda
(or maybe that was just me). Now we've got the paleo revolution,
an all-out war against gluten, and I'm still trying to figure out the
deal with essential oils.

The everlasting truth of who God is and what He does is
black and white, but the interpretation of what it looks like for us
to fit into Christian culture is constantly shifting with the voices
that teach us. God is the solid ground, while the teaching of our

generation is more like the tectonic plates beneath our continents. And this is okay! Seriously, it's beautiful! When we cling to the eternal truths of God's Word and stay nimble to growth in other areas, beautiful stuff happens. For example, hymns! The hipsters are bringing hymns back in full force, but two decades ago? Most people were trashing their hymnbooks and beefing up on praise and worship choruses. They kept worshipping the God of Abraham and Isaac (good!); they just shifted their interpretation of what worship had to look like (also good!).

But when we see those slow-moving plates of wisdom, inter-pretation, and methodology as the bedrock of our faith, we're not on solid ground. It's easier to stand on and build an identity that's based on quotes from humans and man-made systems that aren't as mysterious. There's a reason why a man-made chart explaining salvation is easier for us to follow and comprehend than the Passover story. Our brains love clear communication and easy-to-follow paths, but mystery and miracles don't often follow a chart. There's a deep longing in us to be able to understand something we care about, and while God is not confusing, He is often confounding. This is why it's dangerous for us when we seek knowledge and understanding in an effort to be able to relate, correspond, or fit in with others. Do we want to be tethered to a group based on how much *we* know and whether we comprehend God the same way others comprehend Him, when much of the Bible speaks to God's vastness and how His ways are so much higher than ours?

If we're seeking to learn more *only* so that we can know our place, find our people, and feel like we belong, we've forgotten what it means to be holy women of God. When the pursuit of wisdom becomes about being among the wise, Lord, forgive us. I'm not saying we should constantly play devil's advocate; I'm not saying we should rebel from popular theology just for the sake of rebelling. I *am* saying it's worth an honest look at our pursuit of knowledge to see if we're running after the heart of God in order to know Him better or if we're running after wisdom in order to be seen and known among the wise.

Finally, I'll tell you about one more season of learning that occurred, interestingly, in the first weeks and months following my conversion as a believer. I was fifteen, and I was new to the family of God. One weekend I was whooping it up, drinking and doing drugs, and the next weekend I was squeezing in every single church service humanly possible. I *craved* more of the Lord, and each morning, a few minutes after I woke up, this massive smile would spread slowly across my face as I'd remember forgiveness, grace, purpose, abundance. I think about those mornings every so often, what it was like to remember afresh that your whole life now had purpose and meaning and EVERYTHING WAS GOING TO BE OKAY, after having perceived the exact opposite for so long.

When I first met Jesus, I wasn't a girl who loved doing homework, but I found I did love studying the Bible. I would come home from school every afternoon and set up shop on my bed, eager to get an audience with God. With a fresh notebook, a pen, and my Bible, I'd turn to a section in the concordance, maybe "peace" or "righteousness" or "grace," and I would enter into an hours-long rhythm of looking up and writing, looking up and writing.

I was hungry for the Word of God and thirsty for the Spirit to move in my life. Someone had told me that this crazy fairytale story of redemption was true, so I wanted to know as much as possible. I wanted to dive in deep.

What's interesting about this season is that my idea of deep didn't look like the church's idea of deep. I didn't read any books by long-dead theologians, and I didn't look up any Greek or Hebrew. I wasn't reaching for any big commentaries. There was no memorizing going on, because I was straight-up drinking from a firehose of truth—and who needed to memorize the Bible when you could just read more of it the next day? The Gospels seemed like a novel—like a wild, involved, incredible story—and I just wanted to know what unfolded in the next chapter.

I read the Word of God and I learned like a hungry, believing child. And to be honest with you, I want to be more like that girl every single day of my life. I want to be more like early-Jesus-Jess because she wanted to learn simply in order to *know God better*. She learned as a response to Him and His great love, not in order to be seen as someone who knows God. She didn't seek God to belong; she ran hard after Him because He comforted her with the truth that while she'd never belong on earth, she'd always have a place with Him. She wanted to be learned, because she wanted as much of Him as possible.

DON'T DISCOUNT YOURSELF IN THE FIGHT

Maybe you haven't struggled with any of my particular sinful temptations to make seeking wisdom about me. Maybe it's not that you're wanting to be seen as wise, or striving to fit in to some community. But maybe you also haven't tasted the desire, deep down, for God's knowledge. In Ephesians 6, we're told about a whole armor of God that is designed for us to be able to fight the inevitable spiritual battles of life, and you may have heard it said before that the Word of God is the only offensive weapon that's listed in that armor.

We've got the breastplate of righteousness to protect our identities and the helmet of salvation to keep our minds from believing lies about God, but the Word of God is what we fight with—so we can't actively do damage to our Enemy if we haven't sought to know and understand it, right?

I wonder if a lot of us have discounted ourselves in the fight for various reasons. I wonder if some of you feel like you're not smart enough. I wonder if some of you might feel like being the kind of gal who reads the Bible will make you boring. Maybe you're nervous about what you'll find or what you might be convicted of. Was there something you read or heard was in the Bible that seemed contradictory or unloving and it made you feel like you'd rather not know more? I wonder if, for some of us, it's not that we're seeking knowledge for the wrong reasons but more that we're *not* seeking it for the wrong reasons.

To that potential concern, I want to say: you're safe here. In Jesus's name, I reject and renounce any word spoken over your life (and mine!) that has made us feel unqualified or unfit to dive right into this birthright of ours, this love letter from Him to us. God's Word is our inheritance, and you'd better believe our Father would disagree with anyone who tried to keep us from it, with anyone who tried to keep us from seeking Him.

If you're afraid of what you might find in the Bible, afraid of being confused or confounded, I want to beg you to proceed in faith. To trust the character of God more than what you've previously been able to figure out about Him. We know that He is holy, He is good, He is trustworthy and gracious—so let's dig in to what He has to say, holding those presuppositions more closely than anything else.

LET'S TRY A NEW WAY

Now that we are armed with and held by grace and truth, I believe there is an invitation here from the Lord to seek wisdom and understanding for all the right reasons. We don't need to cross our arms and discount ourselves from the holy pursuit of learning, but we also don't have to continue striving for knowledge if we're doing it for all the wrong reasons. When we recognize our holy standing as daughters of God, I believe we'll be compelled to draw near to the Lord, who responds with the abundance of Himself.

I perceive a new way of studying and gleaning wisdom is emerging among us, but let's be honest—it's not a new way at all. It's new to many of us, a fresh idea in a season of polarizing responses to learning about God. And it's simple, so if you're hoping for some kind of chart or diagram about how to use special highlighters, this is probably not the book for you.

When I think about wise women, the kind who seek knowledge, I always think about Rachael. My girl Rach is a dear friend, and she has this one incredible strength about her. I could talk about it for hours. Here's what Rach does: when she perceives something is wise and helpful for her to do, she does it. She doesn't need to learn the hard way; she doesn't need someone's theory to be proven a million times over. She doesn't make excuses about why the wise thing doesn't work for her, she just does it.

Case in point: lice. A few years ago, each of our kids got a round of lice (thanks, elementary school!) around the same time and we bemoaned how much it stunk, treated our little heads off, and then moved on with our lives. But someone told Rach she should use preventive lice spray, made with essential oils, on her kids' heads. So she does. I went to stay with her one night and I watched in awe as she quietly sprayed each kid's little head with the preventive spray and combed it out. She's been doing it every night for years now. That doesn't sound groundbreaking for some of you, but others of you feel me.

I used the preventive lice spray too for a while. For about two whole weeks, actually, until I decided I didn't need to use it again. And now? Who do you think lives in massive fear of lice invading her home again? Not Rach! Me. Me. Because I don't just do the wise thing and take two minutes to spray my kids' hair every morning.

About a year ago, Rach was spending time with the Lord and she felt Him impress upon her heart that a battle was coming in her life and she needed to be prepared. She's a woman who loves the Lord and loves the Bible, but she didn't have a super regular habit of studying the Word. Well, when she felt God telling her to get ready, Rach started reading the Bible daily to prepare for whatever He was about to do in her life.

She began to wake up thirty minutes earlier every day to read. When it's warm, she sits on her porch with coffee; when it's cold, she sits at her kitchen table. She picks a book of the Bible and reads a chapter or two each day. She prays God will give her eyes to see and ears to hear and she just reads. There are no pens or notebooks nearby, and she doesn't adjust her time with the Word for special occasions all that often. Once I was visiting her (we live about three hours apart), and even though I was only there for about twelve hours, instead of moving her reading time, she invited me to sit on the porch next to her, rocking and reading—soaking up the Word of God.

Rach's story is hers to tell, but I can confirm that she had a

Matthew 7:25 type of year that year: "'The rain came down, the streams rose, and the winds blew and beat against that house; yet it did not fall, because it had its foundation on the rock.'" And Rach kept on rocking and reading, standing on solid ground.

I think the question I get asked most on social media is, "How do you have a quiet time?" And let me tell you, there is not one ounce of me that is annoyed by that question. I love that the women of God are wanting to be intentional and strategic about how to open the Word of God. I love that question. And the good news is, I think the answer is so much simpler than you might think.

Here are a few things that have helped me when it comes to learning from God's Word.

Simply show up

Half the battle is showing up. Open God's Word and read it. Show up to the page and expect God to meet you there. In Isaiah 55:11, God tells us His words won't return void. If you use the wrong pens or if you don't pick a good book to start with, you're still okay! I mean, what does that even mean, anyhow? The whole thing is good. Sure, if you start off in Lamentations, you're going to be in for an uphill battle—but really, the whole thing is good.

Pray for God to meet you there

Ask God to open your eyes, ask Him to give you ears to hear. Ask Him to show you about Himself, with the reminder firmly in place that He is the main character and the entire Bible is about Him. It's about people interacting with Him, but every single story is just pointing us back to His character and the redemptive plan He made for the children He loves so much.

Carry God's Word with you into your day

What about memorizing, you ask? Well, for sure! Do that if it blesses you. Psalm 119 talks about hiding the Word in your heart, but don't feel all stressy about it, okay? I, for one, have a particularly horrible short-term memory. I can remember being three, and I remember every detail of the day my first son was born, but if you ask me what I ate for breakfast today, we're in trouble. Here's what I've learned: if you read the Bible every day, if you learn the character and heart of God and hide that in your heart, it's honestly more effective and powerful than memorizing a string of words without any heart behind them. I'm not saying all scripture memory is bad; I think it's incredibly helpful to have God's sharp words as weapons at the ready. I just think the motivation behind it has to be hiding the knowledge of God in our hearts, not earning medals for memorizing it.

Consistency is key

Jeremiah 15 talks about eating the Word of God, and John 6 talks about Jesus being the bread of life. I'm not going to ever separate the daughters of Christ into snackers and meat-eaters, but you'd better believe I'm going to encourage you to EAT. Eat every day! Eat three times a day if you've got to! Don't fast from Him. Don't stop eating when you go on vacation. Don't stop eating when friends come into town. For the love of God, don't stop eating on stressful days. Those are the times you need the sustenance of His Word the most.

Come because it's a gift

Holy women of God who stand in the righteousness of Christ: don't read the Bible for the wrong reasons, and don't believe the Enemy's lie that it's something you *have* to do to be holy. The Word of God is not a pill to swallow, but a gift to unwrap. This is what we *get* to do, remember? This is our birthright, to seek the face of God and read His beautiful story. This is our inheritance, the Word of God, the Sword of the Spirit, by which we fight the darkness of the kingdom of this earth and partner with our Father to bring victory right where we're at.

Read God's Word first, excellent resources second

Let's not overcomplicate it or overlook it either; let's cling to truth for all the right reasons, and let's allow ourselves to be taught. What about all those other teachings? The sermons, the books, the seminary classes? Those are all beneficial too. I think Matthew 6:33 is so appropriate here: Seek first the kingdom and righteousness of God, and all these other things will be added to you. In this passage Jesus is talking about clothing and food and all the little ways we need to be provided for, but I think it can be applied to our soul needs as well.

Let's read the Bible first, and then add in all the other sources of wisdom after that. Let's approach wisdom that comes from man as just that—wisdom that comes from *man*. Let's read it with eyes that run everything through scriptural filters. Let's read it with the weight we'd give humans, not God. Let's read it to be enriched and to grow, not to critique and find fault. Let's allow the purveyors of wisdom—our mentors, authors, leaders, pastors, speakers—let's allow them to be human and be people who make mistakes. Let's still allow them to be partakers of the gospel, even while we hold the knowledge that the Bible says they'll be held to a higher standard (James 3).

PICK YOUR STYLE OF FIGHTING

We're free to be women who seek knowledge simply to know God better rather than to live up to the standards of others, and we now know that He's given us a mighty tool in the Bible, what Ephesians 6 details as the only offensive weapon in our fight against darkness. But I'm here to tell you, you're also free to find your own style of fighting. You don't have to read the Word of God the way I do, the way your sister does, or even the way your pastor does.

You can read it at night, you can read it in the morning, you can listen to it on audiobook, you can read straight from the Bible without ever looking at a concordance or commentary. You can read it chronologically like a story, or you can go verse by verse. You can use devotionals or download sermons to help you process it. You can read Bible studies, you can try different translations. There is no WRONG way to read the Word of God when you're doing it to seek His face and know Him better. You're safe to pick your style of fighting, as long as you don't miss out on the abundance, on the wisdom, that's been made accessible to you.

From where we stand, drenched in the grace of God and covered in the blood of Jesus, set apart to change the world and determined not to simply be changed by it, let's be women who learn. Let's be women who seek wisdom. Let's be women who love the Word of God.

Let's Study the Word:

LUKE 2:25–38

Now there was a man in Jerusalem called Simeon, who was righteous and devout. He was waiting for the consolation of Israel, and the Holy Spirit was on him. It had been revealed to him by the Holy Spirit that he would not die before he had seen the Lord's Messiah. Moved by the Spirit, he went into the temple courts. When the parents brought in the child Jesus to do for him what the custom of the Law required, Simeon took him in his arms and praised God, saying:

"Sovereign Lord, as you have promised, you may now dismiss your servant in peace. For my eyes have seen your salvation, which you have prepared in the sight of all nations: a light for revelation to the Gentiles, and the glory of your people Israel." The child's father and mother marveled at what was said about him. Then Simeon blessed them and said to Mary, his mother: "This child is destined to cause the falling and rising of many in Israel, and to be a sign that will be spoken against, so that the thoughts of many hearts will be revealed. And a sword will pierce your own soul too."

There was also a prophet, Anna, the daughter of Penuel, of the tribe of Asher. She was very old; she had lived with her husband seven years after her marriage, and then was a widow until she was eighty-four. She never left the temple but worshiped night and day, fasting and praying. Coming up to them at that very moment, she gave thanks to God and spoke about the child to all who were looking forward to the redemption of Jerusalem.

I used to have a great-great-aunt Enid and a great-uncle E.B. Enid and E.B. went everywhere together, and I just thought they were the greatest. E.B. had a player piano at his house, and we'd go every year to see his Christmas decorations and listen to the carols that his piano seemed to pump out magically. Enid always wore bright lipstick, fun baubly earrings, and she was sassy as all get out. I was in my late teens when I finally figured out they weren't married, that Enid was E.B.'s aunt, and he'd promised his mother he'd take care of her. I was a little let down when I realized they didn't have some spicy, fun elderly marriage, but I was encouraged by his faithfulness anyhow.

I gotta be honest, I felt the same way when I realized that the Bible doesn't tell us Simeon and Anna are married. I'd always thought of them as Simeon and Anna, Anna and Simeon, those two faithful sweeties who lived at the temple and recognized Jesus. But when I slow down to read it, I catch the whole word "widow" and realize Simeon can't possibly be Anna's husband. Bummer, but let's get down to business.

I've always been drawn to the story of Simeon and Anna, and I tend to remember them each year when Christmas rolls around and I start thinking about Jesus's early life. These two devoted lovers of God who were rewarded for their consistent presence in the temple have some important lessons for us about being women who want to learn.

In all honesty, it's tough to find good, applicable passages about people who studied the Bible day and night, because the Bible wasn't canonized (or made official) until a few hundred years after Jesus's death. There were scrolls, there were passed-down stories, but Jesus's followers didn't walk around with Bibles or even have one at home. It took some serious dedication to seek wisdom, history, and literature about God in those days.

The synagogue was the main place of learning around the time Jesus was born, and while it looked wildly different than our churches do today, a lot of the rhythms and ideologies are similar. Anyone could come into the synagogue—unlike the temple, where only priests could go—and it was the spot where the followers of God gathered to learn. Appointed leaders would bring the Torah and scrolls of the prophets from the temple to the synagogue to be read, and then an appointed adult would give a short sermon. There would be corporate prayer and worship, but no one was holding their own Bible or taking notes. Listening was the key to learning and retaining knowledge, and it took some dedication. They'd most likely be sitting on the stone floor while the seats were reserved for people of honor.

What I'm telling you is that people like Simeon and Anna, who'd been at this for years, had to work a little harder than we do to seek wisdom and get the gist of what was going on in the kingdom of God. It took some determination and humility to be taught, which is true for us as well, just maybe not in the same way.

SEEKING WISDOM GIVES YOU EYES TO SEE

It's clear Anna and Simeon knew Jesus was the prize. The whole Jewish nation was waiting on a messiah, but we see *their* relief and joy that they got to witness the fulfillment of that promise—not just to them, but to the world as a whole. They weren't pining after vacations, retirement, or the day when they'd finally be honored for their faithful service—they were waiting on and hoping for Jesus.

Have you ever wondered why Simeon and Anna don't seem confused or flustered that it's a child they're meeting instead of some sophisticated king? Throughout Jesus's ministry, people are confused about why He isn't what they expected Him to be, and even His disciples seem to continually be perplexed about what happens when He typically has already told them, THIS IS EXACTLY WHAT IS GOING TO HAPPEN.

Simeon and Anna? They don't miss a beat. Someone shows them a kid, and they throw a party. The Messiah is here.

It seems to me that surely the power of the Holy Spirit is at work, enlightening their hearts and illuminating their spiritual eyes, but I can't help also imagining that their humble and faithful pursuit of knowledge enabled them to be ready for Jesus's arrival. When we give ourselves over to running after wisdom, not for the wrong reasons of becoming puffed up or fitting in, we will find ourselves all the more aware of the character of God and what He might be up to. The quiet, confident alertness that comes from seeking the Lord prepares us for whatever might come; it arms us with the ability to trust His hands and His heart even when things don't work out the way we're anticipating.

This is what people chasing after holiness figure out real quick: when it comes to following a Holy God, you learn to expect the unexpected.

Seeking wisdom breeds familiarity with the heart of God. Simply put, the more we seek to know Him and understand Him, the more we will! Jeremiah 29:13 says that if we seek Him with all our hearts, He *can* be found. I can't imagine anything else I'd like to be written on my tombstone more than *She knew God*. That was Anna's story, and because of it, she's basically my hero. She knew God, so she could witness Him at work. She sought God and gained her treasure. She was familiar with His character, so she wasn't confused when He sent His son as a baby. She believed God, so even after this episode is over, where do we find Anna? Telling more people about what God is up to. Lord, help us see the massive earthly and kingdom benefits we have access to when we seek your face with humility and fervor. Lord, make us more like Anna.

SEEKING WISDOM MAKES US HOPEFUL

I feel wary and cautious when believers get all doomsday and bleak on each other. Here are some things people say, which I believe are not helpful: *The world is coming to an end. We're all going to hell in a handbasket. Culture right now is so messed up, God is going to judge us all and send another flood. Christianity is so threatened; we're the minority, and all the believers will be wiped out in another few generations.*

If you haven't heard any version of those bemoanings, we might just have different sets of Facebook friends. I feel like I can't go a day or two without hearing another believer basically declare, IT'S ALL OVER. THE WORLD HAS WON. But here's the truth: the world has been pretty messed up since Eve ate that apple.

Since the stoning of Stephen in Acts 7, the threat of being harmed for believing in Jesus has been a real and consistent concern for people around the world. Reports tell us that while the numbers of those who profess to know and love Jesus may be slightly decreasing in the US, other places like Asia, Latin America, Africa, and Brazil are all experiencing a revivalistic increase in believers that would blow your socks off. Persecution is not slowing them down; it is adding fire to the flame of the Holy Spirit as hope and life spread wildly across these nations and continents.

The world is a tough and dark place, and I don't believe it's our job as believers to pretend it's not. But the women of God get to be women of hope because we believe God cares, we believe He feels for His people, and we believe Jesus is coming back to set things right.

Anna and Simeon, as they humbly sought learning, didn't

become more discouraged by the days that passed as they waited for the Messiah to come. They never stopped showing up. Their trust and faithfulness were spurred on by the understanding of His character, understanding they received through wisdom and testimony found in Scripture, to the point where their anticipation of His arrival was at a fever pitch.

When we, the daughters of God, seek His face and learn His Word and trust His character, I believe we'll become more hopeful and more anticipatory of His return and His rescue. We'll see people in the correct light, as image bearers of our Holy God; we'll see world events with more clarity; and we'll perceive culture not as barren and broken beyond repair but as reachable and redeemable by the healer of all things. I love how *The Message* version of 2 Corinthians writes this:

> In the Messiah, in Christ, God leads us from place to place in one perpetual victory parade. Through us, he brings knowledge of Christ. Everywhere we go, people breathe in the exquisite fragrance. Because of Christ, we give off a sweet scent rising to God, which is recognized by those on the way of salvation—an aroma redolent with life. (2 Corinthians 2:14–15 MSG)

Do you see how Simeon speaks truthfully about the hardship that's going to come regarding Jesus? He even warns Mary, saying essentially, *This is going to break your heart, Mama.* But he also rejoices! Not because he's met the baby and now he's out of here. He rejoices because he knows that revelation and restoration is on the way, even if it hurts getting there.

We, the women of God, will find hope bursting from our

hearts when we seek His wisdom and find Him. We'll find hope for ourselves and our daily lives, but I think we'll also find the corporate strength to withstand the trials our Enemy has planned for the church at large. I believe we'll find the complexity and grace to weep with those who weep and trust in the truth of redemption at the same time. In Jesus's name, I believe we'll stop seeing the world around us as a hell-bound basket of worthlessness, and we'll start seeing it as a collection of people on the way to salvation, a people who are no further from God than we ourselves once were.

Seeking God and pursuing wisdom doesn't just help us know Him better; it helps us perceive what He's up to, and it enables us to speak hope and life to the world around us when all else seems lost. We're the daughters of God, and we can run hard after Him in humble pursuit, because He has promised that He will be found.

Let's Take It a Little Further

1. What keeps you from feeling the freedom to pursue wisdom and insight about the Lord? Is it fear? Laziness? Doubt?
2. Do you identify with any of the more broken motivations for seeking to learn about God? Which one? What truth do you need to speak to that brokenness in your own life?
3. Do you find your heart more encouraged and hope-filled after spending time with the Lord? Why or why not?

Chapter 7

SHOULDS, COULDS, AND HIGH-PITCHED SQUEALS

HOW HOLINESS SPEAKS LIFE

Read by Meredith Schauer

I don't know how to tell you guys how small and weak the filter is that lives between my brain and my mouth. If something feels even remotely true in my brain, the chances of it making its way out into the world via words is likely.

I've reached a point in my life, which I'll unpack more later, wherein God is helping me see this facet of my personality as a strength, a muscle to stretch and grow. But for the first thirty or so years of my life, it was a liability that kept me and everyone else around me on our toes.

It started when I was little. My mom called them "Jessi-isms," and all throughout my childhood, she joked that she was writing them down, but I'm grateful she didn't. She tells me I was constantly asking blunt questions or making candid remarks about everything I saw, about everything anyone else did.

I am the friend who will tell you you've got spinach in your teeth. If you ask my opinion, you will hear it, and for the love of God, don't ask how my day was unless you want me to tell you something like, "I mean, it was okay. I had a rough meeting, and I've been really gassy lately. My kid was up puking during the night so I didn't get much sleep, and I read this passage in Ezekiel that totally freaked me out and made me question God." To top it all off, I have an overly expressive face—so even when my small brain/mouth filter does its job and I have the opportunity to think before I speak, my big old cheeks and eyes and pursed lips do the talking for me.

What I'm trying to say is that when it comes to considering the power of life and death that resides within our words, I'm totally disqualified and the most qualified all at once. There are plenty of people who have been cut to the quick by the words that have come out of my mouth, and for that, I'm just broken and grieved. Sadder even, you don't have to travel far to find them. My mom, my sister, my husband, my kids—they could all make a list of the things I've said in the past that will never leave their brains. I've apologized and they've forgiven me, but the truth remains: the words were said and their weight lives on, leaving an indentation in the souls of those I love so much.

But! Because of the sobering nature of how I've had to live with my own sin, I'm also the most qualified to write this chapter. Just like we talked about in chapter 3, you can't feel the weight of grace until you've felt the weight of your sin. So I feel like I'm specifically qualified to talk about the merits of the holy women of God speaking life, because as God has convicted me, grown me, and turned me around, I've seen the light. I've seen a whole new way. And slowly but surely, I've learned that while I might not have much of a filter, I have the Holy Spirit interceding on my behalf and helping me change the world around me for the better, not just tear it down with my words.

A CAR AT WALMART

In 2011, Nick and I were in a season that was meager yet sweet. We had one car, a tiny two-bedroom shack, three kids, and just enough money to get by from week to week. There was no extra money to buy coffee or candles, but our life was simple and sweet and there are days when I think I'd move back into that two-bedroom house in an instant. *I could vacuum the whole thing using only one plug.* Who doesn't long for that kind of simplicity?

But because of the one-car situation, I developed a rhythm of running early-early morning errands before Nick left for work if I needed reinforcements for any reason. Milk, diapers, baby wipes—whatever. I'd run to our local Walmart at six a.m. and be back in time for him to take the car for the day.

One weekday morning I was zipping into the Walmart parking lot, ready to skedaddle up to the door and grab my diapers, when I realized I was going down the parking lot lane the wrong way. No panic, because it was six a.m., so it wasn't like I was going to have a head-on collision in the midst of crazy traffic, but I did see one other car coming the right way down the parking lot lane. Still, no stress, I'd just pull to the side and let the driver pass, then I'd get in the correct lane and park.

As the car slowly pulled past me, something crazy happened. I'll never forget it as long as I live. The driver was a woman, about my age, and she was laying on the horn—blasting it long and loud as she slowly drove past my pulled-to-the-side car. Not only was she literally putting all her weight on the horn, her head was almost out the window and she was screaming insults, cuss words, and all kinds of hateful vitriol my way. I had seriously made this gal mad by driving slowly and accidentally down the lane the wrong way at Walmart at six a.m.

I sat there, stunned. I wondered what was going on in her life that made her so volatile. I prayed for her, not because I'm super kind all the time and quick to forgive my enemies, but this was obviously not about me. There was something tragic happening to her, inside her, around her. There was some sort of outside force that made her feel like her only option was to take it out on me.

With goosebumps on my arms and my car doors locked (because come on, that was some scary stuff), I sat in the car and talked to the Lord. It felt like He was quickening my heart to pay attention and to just be still for a moment. I sensed one thing: this aggressive assault, which seemed to come out of nowhere, was familiar to me in an abstract way. The look I saw on my own face, reflected in the rearview mirror, was the look I'd seen on the faces of the people I love. It's not like I go around cursing and screaming at the top of my lungs—but I do this. I speak death, I take it too far, I use my words like a weapon. I let the words of my mouth be separate from the meditation of my heart. I don't use my mouth in a holy way. I take out my emotions on others. But it was never meant to be this way.

POSITIVE REINFORCEMENT

Words satisfy the mind as much as fruit does the stomach; good talk is as gratifying as a good harvest. Words kill, words give life; they're either poison or fruit—you choose. (Proverbs 18:20–21 MSG)

I think we could spend all kinds of time dissecting the ways we all struggle with this. We could talk about cuss words, which are interestingly one of the largest dividing lines in the church. Have you ever thought about this or watched it in communities? This is the kind of stuff I wish I could've written research papers on in college. I think it's so interesting what words different communities consider off limits. Some churches will all but stone you if you use a four-letter word, but you'd better believe they allow some gossip or racial slurs all up in their conversations. In some more modern and contemporary circles, you might find a little more leniency given to certain words that more traditional circles would absolutely consider off limits. Some pastors out and out cuss when they preach, and others call down shame on those who do.

Here's where I'm going with this: none of us is blameless—no not one. Romans 3:10 tells us it's true, and there's no exception when it comes to the power of the tongue. We've all used it for death. Instead of spending any more words calling us out about it, I'd love to just offer some positive reinforcement and encourage us toward a *new way*. I'd like to spend more time talking about how we can speak life, because I think if we spent more of our time attempting to speak life, we wouldn't have to worry as much about the death coming out when we're not being watchful.

I'm going to offer some examples of ways I see the women of God (myself included) struggling here, with some alternatives I'd love us to consider focusing on instead.

SHOULDING VS. COULDING

Shoulds . . . life is full of them. And they'll make you crazy. Some of them are wise and strong and good, solid advice like when your grandmother gives you a life lesson sit-down, and some of them can go right out with the trash. What makes "should" so complicated is that it's always attached to someone else's expectation, someone else's opinion, and if you don't happen to agree or if you fail to meet that expectation, that "should" quickly leads you into shame. In fact, "should" is too often just another way of saying, "shame on you."

Here are some I've heard: You should go to college. You should breastfeed your baby. You should read your Bible. You should clean the sink every night. You should always have more sex with your husband. You should never leave the house without makeup. You should not wear too much makeup. You should buy a home instead of renting. You should have figured out your life by now.

If the Lord had wanted us to live under a system of shoulds, under a proprietary set of potential duties, He would have given us a list and not a love story. In fact, every time the Lord *did* give a set of rules (ahem, the Ten Commandments), it was never meant to be our rescue—rather, the rules were always guidelines to help us live in abundance. The lists God gives are never meant to save us, as Jesus was always His rescue plan. The lists are always for our good, but always given with the foreknowledge that we can't actually accomplish everything on them. God made a way for us to be in relationship with Him precisely because He knew we could not fulfill the requirements to be a holy people. So He gave us His holiness through Christ His Son. Before there was ever a list of rules given to us by God, there was a love story of rescue set in motion.

What we must do as sinners in a broken world (because there's no other option), under the authority of God our Father, is keep on needing Him. We must profess that Jesus Christ is Lord and rearrange our lives to uphold this profession. That's it. The million, swirling "shoulds" out there get complicated and make us think we have to get them all right. We don't—we only need to concern ourselves with this one aim. He does the rest of the heavy lifting, by grace through faith. So let's rewrite those original sentences in a gospel-centered light, with the word "should" thrown far away.

You could go to college. You might be able to breastfeed your baby. You get to read your Bible. You might find peace in a clean sink before you hit the bed. One way to keep a marriage healthy is frequent intimacy, so you could have sex more often if you're in the right emotional and physical space to do so. You can put on makeup if it makes you feel like you've got a pep in your step! You can wear less if it makes you feel fussy. You have options about what kind of housing situation is right for you, and God will give you wisdom there. You're going to need God and His grace for the rest of your life, so there's no rush to have it all figured out.

The more I think on it, the only appropriate use of "should" that I want to be responsible for saying is this: you should cling to Jesus. I feel 100 percent certain that He is the way, the truth, and the life—and you'll find all the possible wisdom you need in Him.

But as for me? I'm going to replace my shoulds with coulds and cans. "Should" says *You have to do this. You don't have a choice. And if you fail, then shame on you.* "Could" says *Well, hey, you have the option to do this. You can weigh it out and decide for yourself.* "Can" says, *I believe in who God says He is in you, and I believe that while you might be human, He is holy, and you're only limited by what He's limited by—which is nothing.* "Can" speaks Philippians 4:13 over my people, telling them, *You can do all this through Him who gives you strength.*

I'm going to speak life over the people around me, and I'm going to stop imposing my experiences on them. I'm going to stop placing pharisaical and man-made (usually Jess-made) expectations on them via the word "should." This doesn't mean I'll stop speaking truth or giving wisdom when God asks me to; it just means I'll no longer take the place of God in their lives, determining what is right and wrong, if God hasn't said it explicitly.

SHAMING DOWN VS. CALLING UP

A few years ago I went to church with one particular woman, and I just about idolized her. She seemed so kind, so strong in the Lord, and she was absolutely winsome. So many women wanted to know her and learn from her. I loved her from afar, too intimidated in that season to go after a real relationship with her, but I did work up the nerve to friend her on social media. I remember feeling so excited when she "approved" our online friendship, that is until I saw one of her more recent posts and felt the wind leave my sails. She'd started the post with something along the lines of, "Who are these women allowing their kids to go see this new Disney movie? Shame on you!" I read it three times through to be sure she wasn't joking. No, no. She was serious. And you know, I'd just taken my kids to see that exact movie, not thinking a single thing was wrong with it. I knew in that moment there was no potential of a great friendship between us, because without even knowing me, she'd shamed me.

That's my paraphrase, for sure, but I know Jesus never shames.

Does that mean He blindly approves of all the things? No, He's not some softy who lets everything go. He stands firm, and

He calls up others to stand firm beside Him. He reminds people of who He is and who they are. Shame puts people down, but holy grace lifts people up by reminding them who they already are. That's the key difference for us, for any daughters of God who are hungry for holiness.

With Jesus as our living example, we get to leave behind our shaming and instead call people up. I believe that when push comes to shove and we have to speak hard truths, we can do so by reminding other believers of where they stand on holy ground. We get to hold the mirror up to their souls and show them that they're image bearers of Jesus Christ. They're saints set apart to change the world. Let's call people up, not shame them as if we are somehow better than them.

CURSING VS. BLESSING

Oh man, if we want to talk about real curse words, let's forget the four-letter ones. Curses in our day have little to do with spells or incantations and everything to do with the proclamations we make over one another's lives.

My husband has never forgotten the day that one of his friends said, "Man—things never seem to work out for you." He remembered it for years to come, and even when logic told him it wasn't true, it seemed like a declaration worth believing. Maybe someone told you that you'd make a terrible mother or it was the joke among your friends that you'd be the last to get married. Perhaps someone constantly reminded you that cancer runs in your family, to the point where it seemed inevitable that you'd one day be diagnosed with it. Maybe someone said you're too sensitive to be in ministry, too busy to be in community, or that big butts run in your family. You might have been told that you never follow through or you can't lead well. It may have been that someone thought you were too old or too young for whatever God had called you to.

Let's not forget the life-stage curses that for whatever reason have become so acceptable in Christian community. These curses disguise themselves as sound advice, but let's take a closer look. We tell brides-to-be at their wedding showers they'd better have all their fun now and spend all the money they can. We tell sweet pregnant moms they'd better get all the sleep they can before the tiny minion steals all rest and relaxation from their lives. We tell mothers of young children they're not enjoying it enough, and it's going to slip through their fingertips. We tell single gals they can't possibly understand what those of us who are married and raising kids do. Lord, have mercy on our sweet cursing selves. No one is exempt from the fury of the women who seem to know exactly what hard things are going to happen to each other.

But have you experienced the freedom and exhilaration of being *blessed* by someone? Like the time someone declared that you were a fantastic listener and you wanted to live up to it for all the days that followed. Maybe someone called out one of your gifts or praised you for your vulnerability. Maybe you've been told you're a loyal friend or a great encourager.

In the final few weeks of my pregnancy with our fourth baby, I was at the mall with my younger three, and I was D-O-N-E. I'm pretty sure I was crying quietly as they played at the play place, with me just kind of haphazardly wiping away my tears. The kids were so stinking hard to manage in that season, and I couldn't fathom why God thought I could handle one more. Also, if you've lived through the last few weeks of a fourth pregnancy, then you know—it's *really* painful. So the gentle crying basically happened all the time, without any warning or effort.

I saw some cute, slightly older moms walking past me with their older kids and thought, "Huh! Must be nice! Look at them walking and drinking coffee at the same time, with their kids who can walk and poop and eat on their own." One of the moms walked past me and then she quickly broke off from her group and ran up to me. She grabbed my arm in a frantic but firm manner, and spoke with authority into my ear.

Her eyes scanned my family sitting before me as she asked, "You got three little kids?" I nodded.

"And you're pregnant with your fourth?" I nodded again.

She looked me straight in the eye as she said, "It's going to be great. You're going to do great. It hurts so bad right now, but in a few weeks, you're going to be so happy. And it's going to be great."

Insert emotional sobbing, am I right? I kept on crying that day, but I believed her. And not only that. I started living like I believed her. Her words became my actions—I lived them out in my actual life. I welcomed that fourth baby with joy and expectancy. It was the easiest transition we had bringing a kid home, and we made up our minds somewhere along the way that it *was* great, even when it was hard.

You'd better believe that when I make hospital visits to new moms or give parting words at graduation parties, baby showers, or bachelorette shindigs, I make sure I find the lady who's being honored and in some way, shape, or form, I tell her firmly, "It's going to be GREAT."

I believe this is the power of words that speak life—they become contagious.

DISBELIEF VS. HOPE

I hope you're beginning to see just how powerful our words can be. And the wild thing for us to know is that even when the words are simple—a hello, a thank-you, a how are you *really* doing?—they carry significance because they are sourced in something deeply eternal.

We can speak words of life because we have unshakable hope. We, the holy women of God, get to offer hope when the world offers disbelief. There's a difference between blind belief and eyes-wide-open hope. It seems like sometimes the church has a hard time finding the balance between doomsday-like proclamations damning our world to hell and naive denial that anything is wrong.

But we get to do it differently by holding grace and holiness together. We get to do it differently by taking off the rose-colored glasses, seeing reality, and speaking truth and hope right into that reality. In our relationships and in our interactions with the world, we get to pry the eyes of our hearts open to see all the hurt and all the pain and all the destruction. And then, without dismissing it and without acting like it isn't there, we get to point to the actual helper, God our Father.

When whole cities are bombed, when politics are going astray, when your daughter doesn't get picked for the school play, when your best friend's husband leaves her for another man, when your mom is diagnosed with cancer—you, holy woman of God, get to hold that hurt and confusion and brokenness and then answer it with truth.

Hebrews 11 says faith is being sure of what we hope for and certain of what we can't see. The Hebrew word for hope in that verse is, or *elpizo*, and it means to actively wait for God's fulfillment of the faith He has inbirthed through the power of His love. Does anyone else want to get that tattooed on their back with me?

Hope means to actively wait for God's fulfillment of the faith He has inbirthed through the power of His love.

Philippians 1 says that we can be confident that He who began His work in us is going to bring it to completion, and Romans 5 says hope doesn't put us to shame because God's love has been poured out into our hearts through the Holy Spirit.

We get to speak life by speaking hope in Jesus to FIX IT. We get to acknowledge that "it" is broken, whatever "it" is on that particular day—big or small. And then we get to speak eternal truth over our lives and everyone around and proclaim, whether here or in eternity, we believe You're going to fix it, Father. We believe You love us and You want good for us, and even though we don't understand why "it" is happening, we trust You. We get to speak life when we speak hope.

HOLDING VS. LIBERATING

The first Bible verse I ever learned was 2 Corinthians 5:17. It says, "If anyone is in Christ, he is a new creation. The old has passed away; behold, the new has come" (ESV). Want to know why that was the first one I memorized and why it's at the top of the list of verses I'll never forget? It's because I'm desperate to believe in the power of restoration that says I don't have to stay the same.

My stepdad says I'm always reinventing myself, and he's probably right. In the past ten years, I've moved from being a stay-at-home mom who never believed she could or should (there's our dirty word) work or have ambitions, to a work-from-home mom who basically needs people to ground her and slow her down constantly. I've gone from being a meat eater to being a vegan and back again. I've had pink hair, brown hair, blonde hair, and everything in between. I've been the running girl, the yoga girl, and I tried for a hot minute to be the weight-lifting girl. In all these years, my sole identity has been that I'm a daughter of Christ, but I *love* the fact that yeah—we're new creations. We can change. He can change us. In silly ways like having pink hair and in big ways like giving us new gifts and skills.

When we think about our words, I believe we get to decide what kind of women we want to be. Do we want to be people who hold others in a certain place or do we want to be the kind of women who liberate those around us with the words we speak over them? When we remind people of who they are or who we expect them to be, are we speaking God's truth or our truth? When we speak about the future of our people, are we making declarations God has spoken or ones our past has dictated? Do we speak liberation over ourselves and others? Do we speak how Jesus would?

It's not something we should do; it's something we get to do. With the rest of the world tearing one another down, we get to look down at where we stand and see that we're the holy women—set apart. The way we talk can be set apart, the way we relate can be set apart, the way we speak, encourage, admonish, and cheer on can be so vastly different from everyone else because we know better.

Because He first loved us, because He spoke truth and purpose over our lives first.

In John 1:12 He calls us children of God.

In John 15:15 He says we are His FRIENDS.

In Romans 3, He says we're justified and redeemed.

Romans 8 says we're coheirs with Christ.

First Corinthians 1 says we're saints!

In 1 Corinthians 6:19 we're told we're temples of the Holy Spirit.

Second Corinthians 5:17 says we're made new in Christ.

Ephesians 2:10 says we're His workmanship.

Ephesians 4:24 says we're righteous and holy.

Colossians 3 says we're chosen, beloved, and dearly loved.

I could go on all day. God is the original and best speaker of life-giving words.

Jesus never shamed us for a moment, and He wouldn't "should" us if He was here right now. We are the women of God, and we get to speak life over ourselves and our world because He speaks life over us.

Let's Study the Word:

LUKE 1:35–56

The angel answered, "The Holy Spirit will come on you, and the power of the Most High will overshadow you. So the holy one to be born will be called the Son of God. Even Elizabeth your relative is going to have a child in her old age, and she who was said to be unable to conceive is in her sixth month. For no word from God will ever fail."

"I am the Lord's servant," Mary answered. "May your word to me be fulfilled." Then the angel left her.

At that time Mary got ready and hurried to a town in the hill country of Judea, where she entered Zechariah's home and greeted Elizabeth. When Elizabeth heard Mary's greeting, the baby leaped in her womb, and Elizabeth was filled with the Holy Spirit. In a loud voice she exclaimed: "Blessed are you among women, and blessed is the child you will bear! But why am I so favored, that the mother of my Lord should come to me? As soon as the sound of your greeting reached my ears, the baby in my womb leaped for joy. Blessed is she who has believed that the Lord would fulfill his promises to her!"

And Mary said: "My soul glorifies the Lord and my spirit rejoices in God my Savior, for he has been mindful of the humble state of his servant. From now on all generations will call me blessed, for the Mighty One has done great things for me—holy is his name. His mercy extends to those who fear him, from generation to generation. He has performed mighty deeds with his arm; he has scattered those who are proud in their inmost thoughts. He has brought down rulers from their thrones but has lifted up the humble. He has filled the hungry with good things but has sent the rich away empty. He has helped his servant Israel, remembering to be merciful to Abraham and his descendants forever, just as he promised our ancestors."

Mary stayed with Elizabeth for about three months and then returned home.

If you ever, ever for a second doubted the power of one woman speaking life to another, you gotta love Mary and Elizabeth's story.

Mary is maybe twelve years old. Maybe as old as fourteen, but potentially just twelve. She's undoubtedly just settling into her incredibly crazy yet typical teenage hormones, she's been promised to a carpenter, and even though these are some big years, she knows what is expected of her and what life is going to look like. Except wait, hold on a second.

The God of her ancestors has been quiet for almost four hundred years. No one has heard from Him. No prophets, no big awakenings. They're waiting on a messiah, and they hear the predictions, but they haven't had as much as a peep from Him. Until an angel bursts into Mary's house. Well, this angel has already visited her cousin Elizabeth and Elizabeth's husband Zechariah, but we don't think Mary knows that yet.

An angel comes to Mary, and Luke finds it worth recording that Mary is FREAKED OUT at first, but Gabriel does this whole monologue promising it's going to be great. Mary asks a really important follow-up question, "Um . . . how though? I haven't had sex," and Gabriel gives a pretty miraculous and mysterious answer. He then tells her about Elizabeth and reminds her again: I promise! It's going to be great! This is great!

The Bible says that Mary responds by saying, "I am the Lord's servant. May your word to me be fulfilled." Which seems sweet, pious, and responsible, right? Can we take a minute and read that the way you might say it if you're a twelve-year-old girl who's just heard from God after four hundred years of silence, a girl who has her whole life ahead of her and is about to seem crazy to everyone—including, for all she knows, her husband-to-be. Mary says a courageous yes to God in a way that will make her a social outcast. It was certainly taboo in that setting to be pregnant and unmarried, but even more than that, it was almost certain she would face an insecure future. Unmarried women who were no longer virgins could not be betrothed. With marriage and family—specifically producing heirs—the pinnacle achievement for a woman in Mary's day, she was at a dire disadvantage being pregnant *before* her actual wedding.

Gabriel's news is eternally beautiful and a blessing, no doubt, but when I read, "I am the Lord's servant. May your word to me be fulfilled," I don't hear any joy or excitement—not in that moment, when the news is so fresh and shocking. I don't hear celebration, frankly. But I hear that she is resolved and that because she loves God, she sure hopes it's all true, or else she is probably just as nuts as she's going to seem to other people.

SAFE TO CELEBRATE

Nick can't help making fun of me when the high-pitched squeal comes out. I see my college girlfriends? High-pitched squeal: "You guyyyyyyys! I missss youuuuuuu!" My sister calls on FaceTime? High-pitched squeal: "Heeeeeey giiiiiiiirrrrrlllll!" I see one of the kids' teachers at Target: "Looooookyyyyy hereeeee, it's Misssss Jessiiicaaaa!" I don't do this all the time, but I'm Southern and silly and feminine, and y'all, sometimes it just sneaks out. I get excited, that's all.

But Lord have mercy, cover your ears when one of my friends is pregnant. I'm the first person you should tell when you find out you're pregnant. FOR SURE. I will do a wild combo of a few different things: jaw drop, maybe physically my whole body will drop to the floor, or maybe I'll only do a minor collapse to my knees. Once I regain my upright position, I'll do a few jiggly dances and awkward hand movements, I'll immediately talk to your belly even if you're only four weeks and three days pregnant, and THEN I will most assuredly give the high-pitched squeal.

You know why? (1) I love babies and pregnancy and always have. (2) I got pregnant eight months into marriage and then had three babies in three years, and I've experienced how it feels when people are less than thrilled to find out you're expecting.

I don't blame a single soul, but by the time I announced I was pregnant with Benjamin, my third, the responses could not have been further from congratulatory. There were a few people who said they were happy for us, but there were even more who expressed how crazy they thought we were. People asked us blunt questions about our birth-control methods and quizzed us on our ability to comprehend how babies are made. Friends who were struggling with infertility simply said, "*Another* baby?" and I saw the pain and frustration in their eyes.

I know what it's like to be pregnant when people aren't necessarily happy for you, and I never ever want another woman to question that I celebrate the life she's been entrusted with. So I'll do my whole high-pitched shebang, and before I leave her, I make sure to intentionally tell her she's going to do great and that she was made for this. I remind her that God picked her for this baby specifically, on purpose, and I tell her she's blessed. Because she is. And Lord, help us not to forget it. If it's our third baby or tenth baby, our adopted babies or our foster kids. Thanks, God, for entrusting us with little souls that we can point to You.

Anyhow, I like to think that Elizabeth came out high-pitched squealing when she saw Mary. I picture this holy and sacred conversation happening with great big smiles on their faces and bellies being rubbed and YOU KNOW THERE WERE TEARS. Elizabeth was eighty-eight and pregnant for the first time, and Mary was in her tumultuous teen years PLUS carrying the Savior of the world. I'm not mad at Luke for leaving out the fact that there wasn't enough tissue in all of the hill country of Judea to absorb their sweet pregnant tears, but I don't doubt that was true for a second.

What Elizabeth does when she sees Mary is so holy and stinking encouraging. She *calls her up* for the challenge ahead. Let's take a look:

"Blessed are you among women, and blessed is the child you will bear! But why am I so favored, that the mother of my Lord should come to me? As soon as the sound of your greeting reached my ears, the baby in my womb leaped for joy. Blessed is she who has believed that the Lord would fulfill his promises to her!" (Luke 1:42–45).

You'll note that there isn't a hint of sarcasm or jealousy in Elizabeth's tone. Here she is, eighty-eight, barren her whole faith-filled life, seeing a twelve-year-old who isn't even married get pregnant. For the record, while both of their pregnancies were nothing short of miraculous, hers is obviously the second most miraculous as Mary didn't even need to have a man involved with her conception, and she's carrying the Savior of the world.

But you know what happens when you believe Jesus is the prize and you've got the prize? You decide you're blessed, and you speak blessing over other people. Elizabeth is over the fact, temporarily, that she's blessed because she's pregnant—now she's just declaring she's blessed beyond understanding because Mary has come, with Jesus in utero, to see her. Elizabeth is freed up to speak mounds of encouragement over her cousin, without any regard for her own self, because she is secure in where her blessedness comes from. She knows cheering on Mary costs her nothing and takes nothing away from her own identity or self-worth.

See, when we're women who live in the world of "get-to's" instead of "have-to's" and "can" versus "should," we're free to speak so much life over other women. When we don't live under obligation or condemnation, but rather dancing in the grace and approval we've been given by God, you'll find us *running* to encourage other women. We won't be hoarding blessing and acknowledgment from others, because we've got all we need. In fact, we've got more than we need, so we'll give some away. When we accept the fact that we live in abundance because we're just so stinking blessed by God's grace and holy call on our lives, we'll lavish that same goodness on everyone else we come in contact with.

Women of God, we are safe to celebrate the accomplishments, achievements, and blessings of others when we know that we ourselves are blessed. We can hold our own heartache, pain, loss, and disappointments in one hand while we pat someone on the back with the other because we know the truth: in Jesus, we are all blessed. We. Are. All. Blessed. Even when we don't feel it, even when we're begging Him for an answer or healing or a gift or a fix, we're all blessed.

NEVER UNDERESTIMATE A GOOD SQUEAL

We took a super close look at what Mary has to say on the front end of that interaction with Elizabeth, so let's take a super close look at what she says *after* Elizabeth's exclamation:

"My soul glorifies the Lord and my spirit rejoices in God my Savior, for he has been mindful of the humble state of his servant. From now on all generations will call me blessed, for the Mighty One has done great things for me—holy is his name. His mercy extends to those who fear him, from generation to generation. He has performed mighty deeds with his arm; he has scattered those who are proud in their inmost thoughts. He has brought down rulers from their thrones but has lifted up the humble. He has filled the hungry with good things but has sent the rich away empty. He has helped his servant Israel, remembering to be merciful to Abraham and his descendants forever, just as he promised our ancestors." (Luke 1:46–55)

Um, excuse me. Is that not the sweetest, most hilarious thing you've ever read? Two paragraphs ago, all she could muster up was: "I am the Lord's servant. May your word to me be fulfilled," and now? She's straight-up preaching! She's like John the beloved disciple, unapologetically declaring God's favor and blessing over her own life. She's preaching about the past and God's faithfulness. She's bringing up Abraham and rulers and the character of God. And then? She knows right where she needs to stay—she camps out at Elizabeth's house where the squealing is plentiful and the conversations are life giving.

If for a minute you have doubted the power of speaking life over another, please consider Mary's outlook before and after encountering Elizabeth. She was alone, afraid, and obedient, yet uncertain. Can you imagine if Elizabeth had said, "Mary, you're not the girl for the job. You're too young, too unknown, too ill-equipped." I'm going to go out on a limb and say we'd have a different story.

But Elizabeth chose to speak life. This is the power we have, friends, when we encounter the people God has entrusted us with. Romans 8:11 says the Spirit that raised Jesus from the dead is alive in us, and goodness gracious, I believe it comes out through our words when we intentionally encourage our people. Have you ever seen someone's soul visibly revived when you've reminded them who they are in Christ or encouraged them to remember what He can and will do for them?

What more holy thing could we do with our days, women of God, than go out into the world and speak life over the people who are listening to us? Our children, our husbands, our sisters, our roommates, our friends, our neighbors, our leaders, our teachers and baristas, the ladies we work out with, people online and in line at the grocery store, and especially, ourselves. What more holy thing could we do than combine the Word of God in our hearts and the Holy Spirit who lives in our minds, and speak life with all we've got?

Never underestimate a good squeal, gals. Never underestimate a good text or a handwritten note or an encouraging coffee date. Don't overlook the power of a passage of Scripture posted on Instagram, a well-timed "God's got this!", or an initiation of some private prayer and exhortation at the end of your church worship time. Let's look down at the holy place where He's put us and remember, we are the women of God and we're here to speak life. Let's ask God to give us the words and stir up our hearts, and let's partner with Him in shifting the perspective of people everywhere.

Let's Take It a Little Further

1. What "shoulds" do you feel the pressure from in your life? What would it look like for you to gently but firmly put aside these expectations from others?

2. What keeps you from speaking life? Try to hone in on the fear or frustration that keeps you from blessing other women.

3. Can you recall a time when someone spoke life over you and it shifted you? What concern did they speak to, and how was their delivery impactful to you?

4. To whom has God called you to speak life today? Make a plan and execute it.

Chapter 8

YOU ARE ALREADY A RUNNER

CLAIMING YOUR IDENTITY AS A WOMAN ON MISSION

Read by Katie Walters

I'm so glad the word *run* is in the title of this book. I absolutely love running. I mean, I LOVE running. But if you've ever met me, or seen the lower half of my headshot, you get why that's a little bit of an interesting factoid. I'm what you call . . . curvy. I'm also fairly short, with a longer torso/top half than my bottom half, so my legs are even shorter than you might imagine for someone my height. To top it off, I've got feet so flat they'd make the Flintstones laugh, and in general, I know I'm not what most people picture when they see a runner. I'm basically the exact opposite of a Nike commercial.

I never really tried to run until I was twenty-six, when I started seeing a counselor for depression. She suggested I try running for the rhythmic alone time and the endorphins, so I did what seemed reasonable and tried one of those "Couch to 5k" plans, where you walk a little and run a little. Walk a little, run a little. And you build up your time until you're eventually running a 5k, or about three miles. It felt like an uphill battle, and I didn't love it, but I wanted to take my counselor's advice, so I kept plugging away and trying to increase the distance I could run. I'd barely made it to the point where I could run one whole mile when something happened that changed my running life forever.

I went on a run with someone else. My friend Kristen was training for a half marathon and she needed to do an eight-miler one day. I was terrified even thinking about it, but there was something electric in my spirit that made me want to join her. I gave all the appropriate warnings about how I didn't think I could run more than one mile, but I'd start with her and see how far I could make it before I had to walk back to where we began. We were only ten feet into our run when I knew I'd be able to make it the whole way. I left all doubts behind and set my sights on finishing all eight miles with her. We ended up running nine miles, and while I couldn't walk the next day, I knew I was hooked. I was a runner.

There were a few things that made running with Kristen so different. Number one is that she's just a cutie and I love being with her. We live in different cities now, and she's added babies and I've added other things, but I'd do just about anything to spend a few hours with her running again. She's gracious and kind and entertaining. We talked as we ran, but we would also let one another breathe and think and be alone.

Number two, Kristen taught me how to pace myself. At first, I was confused why I—the newbie runner—was running faster than my pro friend. I didn't know how fast was appropriate for a beginner, so I was just trying to do what I saw experienced runners do, and that pace was not appropriate for me. Honestly, with my build and my short legs, it might never be physically possible for me. Kristen taught me how to maintain a sustainable pace that would make for a win in the long run.

Number three, as we ran that first day, Kristen told me all her running tricks. They're tools I still use today on every single long run. She taught me how holding your arms as if you're loosely pulling a rope—pulling with one hand, then pulling with the next—helps you get through a tough spot in the run and shows you how much energy should be in your arms. She taught me how to breathe through a cramp. I didn't know you could breathe a certain way to make those bad boys go away, so I was used to just quitting when one came on.

I kept running after that session with Kristen, and while I go through seasons when I don't run as much, I always come back to it and remember: *This is good for me. This is where I'm my most healthy and my most vibrant self.* Running keeps my heart and my mind happy, it keeps my soul light, and I've never ever regretted going on a run.

The main reason I know I'm meant to run is because all the reasons I'd use to excuse myself from running are pathetic and damaging lies. Here are a few of the voices that live inside my head, the ones that occasionally come out when I talk myself out of running:

You're never going to be a tiny human who looks like a runner, so why try? (Truth: the goal of my life is not to get tinier. And I don't run because of how I want to look.)

You work too hard being a wife and mom and writer and business gal! Give yourself a break in this one area and be the kind of girl who doesn't move too much! (I do work hard! But I *get* to work hard in those areas and I'm blessed that God has called me to them. I need to be fit and strong to keep going in what He's called me to.)

The big one: You're just not a runner. You ran a few half marathons, but who are you kidding? You're not a runner. (Truth: what in the actual world is a runner anyhow? Someone who runs. And I run. So go somewhere else, Satan.)

Do you want to know what keeps me running these days? I have the truth and the good experience to look back on, but mostly there's this one random fact I overheard at a party that keeps me going. You'd think the finisher medals hanging in my office would be the ticket, but not for an overthinker like me.

A few months ago, I was in the midst of another conversation when I overheard two people talking about how the human body is more flexible while under the effects of anesthesia. One of them was a doctor who said people can do the full splits when they're put to sleep, even if they aren't all that flexible in their normal day-to-day lives. I tucked that little nugget away in my mental pocket and thought on it through the months that have passed since then. I've done a little research, and different websites say different things. Some debate the full split theory—but almost all of them agree, the limitations we feel when moving our body, even the limitations that are caused by pain, are in our heads, and we can push past them.

So when I run, I don't beat myself up saying, "GO FASTER, DUMMY. DON'T FEEL THE PAIN." But I do ask myself if what

I'm feeling is discomfort that can be pushed past or worked through, or if it's some kind of pain to pay attention to. Almost always, for me, it's pain to work through. And the knowledge that I could potentially run a lot farther if I didn't have my own mind getting in the way, with its doubts and insecurities, calls me to go the distance.

When I run now, I remember that my limitations are largely made up of my own perceptions of what I think I can do, my perception of the pain I'm in, and me allowing fear to grab ahold of me. What's even more interesting is that in the few cases when I've quit a run early, it's almost always because I don't *think* I can finish it—not because I hit a place where I can't keep going anymore.

I believe this is our story as we learn to grow from walking with God to advancing His mission.

The fact of the matter is this: we've been given monumental grace, and God has leaned in toward us, sisters. He hasn't just let us in the back door of the kingdom. He left heaven, coming after us, saying, "I'm not done with you! I have a plan for you! I'm going to redeem your life and give you a new identity!" This is the good news that we dance in; this is the grace that has saved us and set us on solid ground.

And when we look at our feet and see where He's placed us, it's remarkable. When He gave us that new identity, we shifted from being strangers of God to His children to coheirs and ambassadors. He didn't say, "Now follow my rules and live differently so one day you'll be like me." Instead He speaks an astounding new reality over us: "You are clothed now in Christ. You are holy. You are made new." We've already been made like Him, conformed to His image, and we just get to look down at the holy ground we've been placed on and live in a way that agrees with who He says we are with the Spirit's help. Our feet are on holy ground, and we're not just safe from death; we're free to stand firm and live set apart.

But what will we do, as we notice this grace and this miraculous identity work God has done in our lives? Because He didn't just change who we are when He made us new, but He also changed *what we're here for*. Just before Jesus left earth, He gave us a new cause and a mission, asking us to RUN to the world and tell them what God our Father has done for us. The question isn't if we've been given grace or if we've been given new holy identities, the question is what will we do with the truth that we have received both of those things? Will we stay here, continually looking down at the ground we've been purchased to? Or will we get ready to run?

It seems most of us are believing we're not the mission type because we have some kind of false picture in our head about what that means. Maybe you're the type that guns it out of the gate too fast in a way that burns you out quick on service and ministry, because you're comparing your call to your perception of how fast and far other people run.

Or maybe you're the solo runner type. It seems many of us don't know how to run in groups, we don't know how to run together, so we get lonely and we believe the lie that leadership and mission will always be a solitary duty. We're not informed about the tips and the tricks either, because we're not humble enough to ask, or because those going before us aren't giving us the wisdom we're desperate for. We're continually discounting our own ability to run on mission because we're too busy believing the doubts, limitations, and restraints that live not in reality but in our own heads.

Or maybe you're like me and have never felt like a "real" runner in the first place, so you've barely gotten started. We do this all the time—disqualifying ourselves before the race ever begins, believing that never getting started is better than falling flat on our faces.

Anyone else ready to remedy that? Have we talked enough about grace and our holy standing with God that your feet are itching and your hands are quivering and the words are just piling up in your throat, ready to spill out? If you're already living on mission in a life-giving way, are you ready to help lead the rest of our generation to their battle positions in the kingdom?

We have danced in His grace and we are standing on holy ground, and for goodness' sake **we are runners**. God called us that, and what He has spoken over us, no one can argue against.

YOU ARE ALREADY A RUNNER. YOU ALREADY HAVE A CALLING.

What a great time to be women in the church. I don't believe we've gone the full distance in the American church to embrace women, to equip them and utilize the gifts God has given them for the glory of God and the good of the saints, but I believe we're making progress, and we continue to make progress.

So I'm grateful that stay-at-home moms, college students, single women, grandmothers, and daughters alike are asking this question: *What is it that I'm called to and how do I know what God has equipped me for?* I do think, however, that the answer has the potential to be simpler than we'd like it to be, and I believe we've been staring at it for quite some time.

Are you ready? Here's our mission:

> Then Jesus came to them and said, "All authority in heaven
> and on earth has been given to me. Therefore go and make
> disciples of all nations, baptizing them in the name of the

Father and of the Son and of the Holy Spirit, and teaching them to obey everything I have commanded you. And surely I am with you always, to the very end of the age." (Matthew 28:18–20)

Let's get something on the table before we move any further. I'm not sure what you've been told or what the flavor of your particular Christian community is like, but if you've believed, even in the back corner of your heart, that women were not included in the Great Commission, you've been misled. You are no second-class citizen in God's kingdom. Women were not merely onlookers in this story, and you're not excluded from this mission today.

Women were referred to as disciples in the New Testament, and they were referred to as disciple-makers in the New Testament. In fact, in the book of Matthew (where this most famous passage describing the Great Commission is found), from the time of Jesus's crucifixion to His ascension, women are mentioned as disciples four times more than men. The only person referenced more than the female disciples in that stretch of Scripture is Jesus Himself.

So women of God, here is your primary calling: **Go and make disciples**. Teach them what you know. The entire Trinity is on your side, and they'll keep helping you until you get to heaven.

There are a few different versions of the actual word *calling* used in the New Testament, and while the word *calling* isn't in this passage, I think the word that most relates to the Great Commission is: κλῆσις, or *klesis*, which means an invitation or a summons from God. This is an invitation into abundant mission that is extended to *everyone*, and this, friends, is the largest part of our calling that I believe we would like to gloss over and move past, or perhaps even discount ourselves from.

Here's a response I think a lot of us might have to the Great Commission:

"Yeah, yeah. I know about THAT, but I mean *what* am I supposed to do and *how* am I supposed to do it? I can tell I have gifts I'm supposed to use. Should I start a business or begin writing a book? Should I start a book club or a nonprofit? What is my actual calling? And don't you know how frustrating and hard it is to see other women so sure of theirs when I'm not sure of mine?"

I think that when we respond like this, we're probably missing the depth of the mission we've been called to. This is a little bit like obsessing over what kind of running clothes you're supposed to wear and missing the beautiful fact that you've been made able to run in the first place. This is the danger zone we step into when we confuse the purpose of our mission, thinking it's about ourselves, and we miss the holy trust that's been handed to us.

He's called us disciple-makers, coheirs with Christ, ambassadors who are able to point people toward the marvelous light that will save them, free them, and give them eternal life. We've been handed the keys to the kingdom, but we're maybe feeling tender about what neighborhood we've been placed in.

The thing is, making disciples right where you're at is often heavy, overwhelming work. Making disciples right where we're at, for some of us, will take so much time and energy, we might not have the margin for any "extra callings" in the kingdom. Mothers, telling your children about the God who made them, who loves them and made a way for them, pointing them on the path to being disciples? Hard stuff. Loving your coworkers and friends and community members and walking the delicate path of ministering to them and keeping your soul intact at the same time? Not so easy. Being full present where God has placed you, spreading His fame and teaching His truth, and baptizing people as you go? This is ministry, this is mission, this is our calling, and it's nothing to gloss over.

When I start to feel this yearning in my heart, this desire to understand my exact calling or my next project, it's usually time for me to take a hard look at my current day-to-day life. Am I actively working to make disciples where I'm at? Am I noticing the lost around me, fighting in prayer for them? Am I encouraging those whose relationships with God are newer than mine, the college gals at my church or my sons and daughters? Am I taking note of what they seem to be struggling with, carrying their burdens with them, sacrificially loving them as they grow? For that matter, am I handling my own discipleship well? Seeking wisdom and truth from those who are wiser or further along than me? Am I living as a healthy disciple as I seek to make other disciples?

These are hard questions to ask ourselves, but such prudent ones to pause on before we move on to asking God for any extracurricular callings. Luke 16:10 says, "Whoever can be trusted with very little can also be trusted with much, and whoever is dishonest with very little will also be dishonest with much." Likewise, I love how Zechariah 4:10 encourages us not to despise the days of small beginnings. I've found that women who start with making disciples right where they are, in a healthy way, often don't have time to long for that extra special add-on calling. They feel overwhelmed and grateful for the work right in front of them as it comes and changes.

You have a calling. It's the Great Commission. It's to make disciples, teach them God's truth, and remember that the entire Trinity is with you all the way. Jesus has promised to be your strength when you ultimately come up weak (2 Corinthians 12:9), the Holy Spirit is committed to never leaving us and always bringing us peace (John 14), and the Father sings over us and delights in us as His kids, the ones He can't get enough of (Zephaniah 3:17). You're already a runner. Not because of how far you've run or how you're made, not because you hang out with runners or because you have the right clothing. You're meant to run on mission because God called you a disciple-maker when He commissioned you. And no one can call you otherwise.

Then there's another big question this mission raises. I've asked it myself, and I bet you're asking it too:

"I hear Matthew 28, but I don't know that it applies to me. Isn't that for pastors and evangelists? Wasn't He talking just to the apostles? How can I even do that in my daily life?"

No.

No.

By the power of the Holy Spirit and the grace of God alone.

My beautiful, loving, amazing sisters in Christ: please, for the love of God, don't miss what I'm about to say. If we were sitting together, I'd have all the tears and my hands smooshed against your cheeks. Even those of you who aren't the touchy-feely type, don't put it past me—I've done it before.

You were saved by grace, plucked out of darkness, and called into a purposeful life. You are covered in the blood of Jesus and are held firm by the righteous covering of His identity that surrounds you. You get to DANCE in the grace of God that has set you free and created a path to eternal liberty for the rest of your life. Because of the love of God your Father, the work of Jesus on the cross, and the Holy Spirit that is moving and acting inside of you, you have dominion over death, darkness, despair, brokenness, and pain. Even while you live in this fallen world and feel the effects of sin all around you, YOU ARE VICTORIOUS. Christ in you has made it so. You get to *dance*. Because grace has shattered the curse over your life. Whatever lie the Enemy of your soul has implanted in your heart to tell you that you shouldn't be dancing, well that lie is wrong. **You get to dance.**

You were not just saved from darkness and despair; you were saved *to* a place of holiness and righteous calling. You were beckoned by the God of the universe, who has saved a seat for you among the most upright saints, sons and daughters of God. When you look down at what's beneath your feet, you should find a solid rock, an everlasting love, and a firmament that will last long past anything you can comprehend or see. You were made holy when you believed in Jesus by grace, through faith, and you are as holy as you'll ever be. That doesn't mean you have to live holy or that you should live holy to earn some kind of merit with God; it means you are already good in His eyes and you *get* to respond to His holy call with abundant obedience. You weren't just let in the back door because He was feeling sorry for you. You're a holy daughter of God, given a seat of honor at Christ's table, and you get to act like one.

Now, my precious friend, when you take in those two facts full-on, *why* and *how* could you discount yourself from a life of ministry? What more could you want than the eternal stamp of approval from the God of Abraham, Isaac, and Jacob? What more could you need than the spurring truth of the grace that's been lavishly poured, dumped, heaped on you since the moment God chose you and invited you into His family? What in the world are you waiting for?

It is because I love you that I tell you, friend: It is time to stop making excuses and run. It's not that I'm worried you're going to do it wrong, it's not that I'm worried you're going to disappoint God. I'm terrified that you're going to get to heaven and feel the ache of what could have been had you only believed God when He called you a runner.

Let's take Him at His Word now, compelled by grace and seeing the holy space He's called us to. And let's run.

AND ALL THESE THINGS WILL BE ADDED TO YOU

So let's say we're women who are ready to stop overcomplicating calling and ready to grab hold of what He's asked us to do right where we're at. How do we do that? How do we not get overwhelmed by that task? How do we know when it's time to move on to something else? I'm so blessed to tell you (and remind myself) that He gave us some straightforward instructions about that.

Matthew 6 is one of my favorite chapters in the Bible, right in the middle of Jesus's Sermon on the Mount. When I go through dry spells in my faith, I usually find I've stepped too long away from the direct words of Jesus. I'm also so encouraged by His gentle instruction and wisdom for us. I shake my head and remember, He wants GOOD for me. He wants me to enjoy running in His kingdom. He prayed for me (John 17) and gives a good amount of tips and tricks to keep me healthy and on mission.

And for those of us who tend to worry about our hair and clothing (you know, basically all of us) there's this sweet little snippet at the end of Matthew 6 that is filled with encouragement and challenge, a reminder to keep the main thing the main thing:

"And why do you worry about clothes? See how the flowers of the field grow. They do not labor or spin. Yet I tell you that not even Solomon in all his splendor was dressed like one of these. If that is how God clothes the grass of the field, which is here today and tomorrow is thrown into the fire, will he not much more clothe you—you of little faith? So do not worry, saying, 'What shall we eat?' or 'What shall we drink?' or 'What shall we wear?' For the pagans run after all these things, and your heavenly Father knows that you need them. But seek first his kingdom and his righteousness, and all these things will be given to you as well. Therefore do not worry about tomorrow, for tomorrow will worry about itself. Each day has enough trouble of its own." (Matthew 6:28–34)

In this passage, our sweet Savior is essentially saying: CHILL. I give the flowers stuff to wear and they look pretty. I'll take care of you. You just keep seeking My kingdom—keep wanting more of Me, keeping running after the things I care about, and I'll add on all the extras you're going to need. Stop worrying about what's next—today is enough. Right where you're at, seek Me and My glory, and you'll be good.

This particular paragraph is about clothes, but most of what comes before this is about kingdom work. Matthew 6 begins with wisdom about giving to the needy and continues on into well-known teachings about prayer, fasting, and seeking the kingdom. So I think this strong advice from Jesus to focus on seeking the kingdom first is good for us to take in and apply elsewhere when needed, right?

Here's what I'm getting at. We talked about the general calling found in the Great Commission, the κλῆσις, or *klesis*, an invitation or summons from our Father. But I happen to know that a lot of us are still getting tripped up on the secondary issues of calling, the questions and concerns rolling around in our heads regarding exactly what it is we're supposed to be doing for God, with God, in His name.

I asked a few women from my personal life what concerns or questions they had regarding calling, and here's what they said:

> I struggle with the idea that calling is this big dramatic thing I'm missing out on. If I haven't experienced some kind of emotional event, am I still called?

> I struggle with finding the delineation between work I get paid for and calling. I find myself believing they need to be one and the same. I'm searching for a calling and a career wrapped up in one.

> I struggle with the legitimacy of calling—how do I know if something I feel called to do is God's will?

> I find myself doubting if callings really exist. Isn't it something we just claim to chase while we ignore our other responsibilities?

> I find myself doubting things God has called me to when they get hard or when others discourage my work. It already feels unclear, and then I wonder if we'll ever fully know what we're called to because we're humans and God is God.

These are big questions, and ladies, we live in a big world where even more questions and concerns regarding calling might exist. I imagine some of you feel called to things that women in our church communities might be discouraged from participating in, and Lord knows navigating that kind of tension takes a lot of wisdom and humility. I'm willing to bet that a few of us have felt called to something and then failed at it, leaving us questioning how intimate with the Lord we are or whether or not He even exists in the first place. I know there are more than a few of us who look down at the place we're in and don't see gifts, or talent; we don't *feel* special or feel set apart by God. Instead we're pretty sure we were passed over in the calling department, or at the very least we believe we did something along the way to excuse ourselves from whatever God had planned for us.

There's not an easy answer here. There is no map in the back of the Bible to help us figure out what we're called to. There are a handful of verses that encourage and direct us, we've got the Holy Spirit, and we've got wise people in our individual communities who can help give us insight—but for the most part, this is no easy thing to sort through. So I'll do what I do best when things get murky: hop into a story!

In the winter of 2008, my husband sat me down and told me God had called him to plant a church that would plant other churches. The church would be called Gospel Community, and our first location would be in Boston. At the time we were living just outside Seattle, Washington, and he was in the process of interviewing for what I believed was his dream job (our dream job!) at our home church. We were pregnant with our third baby in just under three years, and the only thing I'd ever told Nick I didn't want to do in ministry was be a church planter's wife.

When he unloaded the news on me, Seattle was at the beginning of a freak snow storm, and we were stuck together in the house for several days. I don't think I spoke to him for almost four days. I'd alert him to dinner being ready, I talked to the kids and played with them, but I was so mad and so frustrated that he would drop this horrible bomb of a calling on me, I couldn't bring myself to speak to him.

Somewhere along the way, I relented and reluctantly began to help him plan our move and church launch. We made a logo, he began fundraising, we talked to wise people and got counsel from all different areas. He traveled to Boston multiple times, coming back with vigor in his step and a smile on his face, sure this was where God wanted him. Once I even traveled to Boston with him, and we did a prayer walk around the neighborhood we planned to move into. We stood on top of Beacon Hill, looking out over the city, and I felt it in my bones: calling.

I was moved to tears thinking of the people, and I felt a longing in my heart to be able to tell them how much Jesus loves them. Even though it made no sense, even though they looked like wise giants in the land and we felt like uninformed kids, there was a desire that could have only come from God to do something that was only for His glory. I suppose that's my personal definition of calling, of what comes after our initial Great Commissioning into making disciples right where we're at. I believe with all I've got that in addition to the general invitation we have into kingdom work, there are oftentimes direct summons that come from the heart of God to His people, and they look like a proposal that could only have been from Him and can only be for His glory.

I'll cut to the chase and tell you this: we never moved to Boston. In fact, we never even visited again after that tearful moment looking out and praying over the city. Our plans continually fell through to move there, God made a way for us to move to the least likely place we ever thought we'd find ourselves, and it just didn't work out.

I'm an emotional gal, and I can get caught up in feelings, but I knew what I sensed about Boston wasn't just pure emotion. And my husband? He's the least of the emotional ones and never gets caught up in anything, so I know there was something at the heart of that calling that was real and specific and from God. I don't know why it was there, and I don't know why it went away. I don't think we'll ever move to Boston, but goodness gracious have we spent days of our life praying for its people. We keep up with other church planters there, and we still find ourselves feeling like we're part of a city we've never lived in. My husband has a Boston area code for his cell phone even though we never had a Boston address.

What I *do* know is that we sought the kingdom of God and resigned ourselves to whatever ministry would look like for us. We relented, submitted, and held our hands heavenward, releasing our plans and asking for only His to go forward. I think we could still be sitting in counseling today, sorting through our confused feelings about how life didn't go as planned, but instead we decided to pick ourselves up right where God placed us and keep on making disciples.

I think we, sisters, could dig into God's Word here, and I could try in my own might to make you a little chart to figure out what your calling might be. We could make maps of the gifts He's given you and we could talk about your five-year goals, the visions He's given you, and the prophetic words that may or may not have been spoken over where you're going.

Or instead, I think we could charge one another to make disciples where we're at, seek first the kingdom, and run on mission without worrying or overcomplicating the idea of calling. I believe we can ask the Holy Spirit for wisdom, listen to the wise counsel of the people around us, line up our ideas and plans with the Word of God to make sure they're sound, and just give it a shot. You think you might be called to write, sing, lead, go, stay, start, quit, paint, teach, or serve? I say give it a shot. Ask the Holy Spirit, ask wise people around you, make sure it's in line with Scripture, and then give it a try.

When we seek first the kingdom, when we put all our chips on just wanting to see His name and His fame advance, we cannot thwart any good plans He has for us. We cannot step out of His will or His boundaries for our life, and there are multiple Scriptures to hold us in safety here: Proverbs 19 says that many are the plans in a man's heart, but the Lord's purpose prevails. Proverbs 21 says that no plan can succeed against the will of the Lord. Isaiah 14 says that God's plans and purposes always prevail.

My sweet friend, your power is so much smaller than His, and that is a beautiful thing.

Your trying, your purposes, your stepping out into the potential of calling is so NOT dangerous when your eyes are on Him and you are seeking first the kingdom of God. You cannot screw up your life, and you cannot screw up His plans.

Women of God, let's remember that when God called us to run on mission, He equipped us for the job. You are a runner!

He's already won all the medals and all the awards. He's already finished the race. We've just inherited His identity, which invites us into this great mission, and it's our joy to get to run toward Him, bringing as many with us on the way as possible. Let's worship God and seek His kingdom, not worshipping the idea of calling or the invitations and gifts He may give each one of us. Let's keep the main thing the main thing. Let's keep our baggage light, and let's run on mission together for the sake of our Savior.

Let's Study the Word:

HEBREWS 11:24-40

By faith, Moses, when grown, refused the privileges of the Egyptian royal house. He chose a hard life with God's people rather than an opportunistic soft life of sin with the oppressors. He valued suffering in the Messiah's camp far greater than Egyptian wealth because he was looking ahead, anticipating the payoff. By an act of faith, he turned his heel on Egypt, indifferent to the king's blind rage. He had his eye on the One no eye can see, and kept right on going. By an act of faith, he kept the Passover Feast and sprinkled Passover blood on each house so that the destroyer of the firstborn wouldn't touch them.

By an act of faith, Israel walked through the Red Sea on dry ground. The Egyptians tried it and drowned.

By faith, the Israelites marched around the walls of Jericho for seven days, and the walls fell flat.

By an act of faith, Rahab, the Jericho harlot, welcomed the spies and escaped the destruction that came on those who refused to trust God.

I could go on and on, but I've run out of time. There are so many more—Gideon, Barak, Samson, Jephthah, David, Samuel, the prophets. . . . Through acts of faith, they toppled kingdoms, made justice work, took the promises for themselves. They were protected from lions, fires, and sword thrusts, turned disadvantage to advantage, won battles, routed alien armies. Women received their loved ones back from the dead. There were those who, under torture, refused to give in and go free, preferring something better: resurrection. Others braved abuse and whips, and, yes, chains and dungeons. We have stories of those who were stoned, sawed in two, murdered in cold blood; stories of vagrants wandering the earth in animal skins, homeless, friendless, powerless—the world didn't deserve them!—making their way as best they could on the cruel edges of the world.

Not one of these people, even though their lives of faith were exemplary, got their hands on what was promised. God had a better plan for us: that their faith and our faith would come together to make one completed whole, their lives of faith not complete apart from ours. (MSG)

For these last few chapters, I'm going to do less talking about Scripture, and I'd like us to get into the rhythm of taking action based on what we read in God's Word. I love the above passage from Hebrews 11 because it enables us to see what God can do with the children of God when they stop discounting themselves as the runners He's made them to be.

I'd love for you to look back on your life with spiritual eyes and write a Hebrews 11-type story of your life so far, including where you're at right now. What has God rescued you from? What has He redeemed you from? What has He gifted you with? How are you currently believing Him?

If defeat or discouragement has entered your mind because you don't feel like you have a story to write, my encouragement for you is this: write a new one. Still do some writing, but you don't have to talk about the past at all. Start today and talk about where He is pointing you right now. Write a story about how you're going to choose faith and step into the life of running that He's set before you.

Don't be afraid to get it wrong. Share it with a friend and encourage her in her own story. If you can't find a single friend to read this book with you, hop on dancestandrun.com and we'll give you a way to read with other women, to process grace, holiness, and mission together.

Let's Take It a Little Further

1. What's your story? Where were you before God, and where are you now? Where has He taken you? What fruit has He grown in your life?

2. Is there anything keeping you from taking your God-given place as a runner on mission? Confess it to God first, and then confess it to a friend. Is there anything in your life hindering your ability to run well for the long haul? Confess it to God first, and then to a friend.

Chapter 9

ONE FOOT IN FRONT OF THE OTHER

EVERYTHING I'VE LEARNED ABOUT RUNNING WELL

Read by Hannah Arnold

Do you see what this means—all these pioneers who blazed the way, all these veterans cheering us on? It means we'd better get on with it. Strip down, start running—and never quit!

HEBREWS 12:1 MSG

About two years ago I started a gang. A girls' running gang. Kind of like a biker gang, but we looked a lot less ominous. It was made up of a rotating group of women, maybe eight in all, and most Saturday mornings in the fall and winter we would run all around Charleston. Some of us were moms getting back into shape after babies, some of the gals were in college, some were young adults not yet married or having kids. The lengths of our runs always varied—on a certain day one gal might be running six miles and another girl might be running twenty, but we always started at the same spot and kept tabs on each other. Some were fast runners and some were slow, some had been training for years, and there was the occasional gal on her first run.

We cheered on one another and commiserated about our achy legs. We brought snacks for each other and scouted out bathrooms on our routes to keep each other from being too uncomfortable. We were a sweet little running gang, full of freedom and purpose, stomping all around this city with our Nikes on.

If we're going to run on mission, we've got to go in a group. It's messier, and it takes more application of the gospel. We'll need to repent more often and check on each other; we'll spend time caring for each other—sometimes almost as much as we care for the people we're ministering to, but we'll be so glad we went together.

In the last chapter we jumped headfirst into the truth that we are already women who get to run on mission, there are none of us who are discounted from ministry, and there are none of us who get to bypass disciple-making either. In this chapter, we're going to hit just a few tactical principles for what it looks like to live out our callings. I believe this starts with running together.

While we're called to ministry and mission, and it's clear we're promised the gift of the Holy Spirit, we're *not* promised ease or pain-free disciple making. We're kind of promised the opposite since we're placed in this world with its own earthly king and dominion—Satan, the Enemy of our souls, prowling around with his own forces trying to thwart the gospel work we're called to. As much as I believe that a life of mission is one of abundance, I know firsthand that a life of mission is also one of challenge, heartache, and frustration.

When you come against the schemes of the Enemy, you'll need

community to help fight and intercede for you. When you hit pockets of loneliness and discouragement, you'll need women running along beside you to cheer you on and remind you of the prize. It will be beneficial to have other disciple-makers reminding you of your identity in Christ and the blessings of His glorious riches, which are at your disposal. We all need the occasional poking and prodding to get going and get back up after a tumble, like an annoying text from your running group when the bedcovers feel warm and your eyelids feel heavy.

I need women in my life to tell me my mission matters and that it's worth fighting for, and I need women in my life to tell me when I'm taking it too seriously and need to let loose and get back to dancing. I need men and women in my life to help me ask hard questions about where I'm putting my time and my money, whether or not I'm remembering the holy ground I stand on. I need a friend to celebrate with me when God uses my service to make a new disciple, and I need friends who will sit with me as I cry or pray over the souls who are still far from Him. Even this book! I asked a team of women to pray with me before I ever wrote a single word. I updated them periodically, begging them to pray with and for me and for all of you who would read it. Then I asked each one of them to read at least one chapter and give me honest, hard feedback. I literally could not have written this book without them, and you definitely wouldn't have wanted to read it if they hadn't weighed in, either.

If we're going to run far, we've got to run with people. We've got to stop worrying about who looks like a natural runner, who seems to go a little faster, and who is more experienced. It's not about the performance, it's about the process. It's not even about the runners, it's about Who and what we're running to: the kingdom of light, the lover of our souls, the creator of the universe. Let's run with people, and let's make sure we're continually growing our running gang, making room for new women along the way.

DRESS THE PART

We have a mission, right? So we need to dress the part. I mean, consider the alternative: no one wants to run naked!

Listen. I feel great about who God made me to be, and I've made peace with the jiggles and the wiggles and the wrinkles and creases. It is what it is, this body of mine; it gets done what it needs to get done. I believe in the beautiful freedom to enjoy our bodies in a godly way that comes in marriage, and my man has seen all the inches and parts of me there are to see, probably many more of the parts than I've seen myself. (Praise God for sex! Wait until marriage for it—it comes with so much more beauty and blessing than you can imagine!) But as comfortable as I am with my body, I cannot imagine ANYTHING more terrifying than being forced to run naked.

The idea of RUNNING naked, jiggling all the things, with other people watching? Yes, I'll just die please, thanks. Not only does that sound terrifying and soul-shattering, it also sounds painful as the jiggles and the wiggles don't feel so comfortable when experienced at high speeds with intense impact.

Here's what I'm saying: If you're trying to run without getting dressed, you're making a huge mistake. If you're trying to be on mission without putting on the daily truth of God's Word, receiving

His grace and compassion for you, soaking up wisdom because you get to, and fueling your spirit with worship and prayer—you're going to regret it.

Go with people, run on mission in community, and put your clothes on. Every single day. Get dressed in the full armor of God so you can keep going and you don't feel ashamed and you don't get sore from things moving all around that needn't move around.

Let's go straight to Ephesians 6 to see what kind of clothes we need to put on:

> Finally, be strong in the Lord and in his mighty power. Put on the full armor of God, so that you can take your stand against the devil's schemes. For our struggle is not against flesh and blood, but against the rulers, against the authorities, against the powers of this dark world and against the spiritual forces of evil in the heavenly realms. Therefore put on the full armor of God, so that when the day of evil comes, you may be able to stand your ground, and after you have done everything, to stand. Stand firm then, with the belt of truth buckled around your waist, with the breastplate of righteousness in place, and with your feet fitted with the readiness that comes from the gospel of peace. In addition to all this, take up the shield of faith, with which you can extinguish all the flaming arrows of the evil one. Take the helmet of salvation and the sword of the Spirit, which is the word of God. And pray in the Spirit on all occasions with all kinds of prayers and requests. With this in mind, be alert and always keep on praying for all the Lord's people. (Ephesians 6:10–18)

Let's start with pants. This passage doesn't mention pants, but it does mention a belt, and that's good enough for me. You've got to be hearing truth, day in and day out. Truth from God's Word, truth from the people around you, and please don't forget that you've got to be hearing truth from YOURSELF. If you read Scripture faithfully and hang around lots of wise people and still sputter lies at yourself day in and day out, my bet is you'll still be hearing more lies than truth. Listen to your own self talk, find out if it's rooted in Scripture, ask the Holy Spirit to convict you, and open your eyes to the messages you're receiving and the ones you're doling out.

The breastplate of righteousness is what we're going to call the sports bra of God's grace, and I think Jesus would be so blessed by this analogy. Let's remember that we're not righteous by our works alone, but by His goodness imputed to us on the cross, and it's only in this truth that we can stand firm and not be vulnerable to attacks of any kind. Our hearts are secure when wrapped tight in His grace that we've received by faith, the same grace that was initiated by His love. Remind yourself daily of where your righteousness comes from and what that miraculous implantation of identity calls you to.

Put your shoes on, girl, the ones that are ready to go at any moment because they are enveloped in the peace that only Christ can offer. These legs are ready to run on mission because they remember who is in control and who all this is for. These feet aren't shifting nervously or retreating when it gets hard, because there is a daily renewal and stomping declaration that their mission is about the kingdom expanding and nothing else. These feet know that Christ already won the war; this is just another battle, and the victory is always His.

We're going to call that shield of faith the sunscreen you need before you go out for a long run. Lord knows it's going to get warm, and the heat is going to come, but you're not going to be burned when your faith is in the One who has called you to run. The helmet of salvation, the remembrance of your testimony and your joy in the gospel that saved you is going to keep your mind right, your thoughts clear, your theology submitted to God.

And girl, you know what's coming next. I don't know what to call the sword except to call it a sword. There's no modern equivalent to running here, but the mission we're on is just not everyday, ordinary stuff. Our only offensive weapon is the sword, and if we're not taking advantage of it, we're covered and defended but we can't do battle. Read the Word, women of God. Because you get to. Because life is a good, hard fight. Day in and day out, pick up your sword so that you can run well and fight hard.

I've found that for me, doing battle in the day-to-day is mostly fighting what I feel with what I know. I'm a feelings girl through and through, there's no getting around it, and I don't think our feelings are bad or dangerous or even worth ignoring. But I think we *fight* by saying one simple sentence: I feel _____, but I know _____. Let me give you some examples:

I feel tired, but I know God has promised to be my strength.

I feel offended, but I know my life is hidden with Christ.

I feel confused, but I know God has promised to give me wisdom.

I feel alone, but I know God has said I'm never alone.

I feel defeated, but I know that victory was already accomplished on the cross.

We walk into a world filled with spiritual battles, physical work, hardships, pain, and confusion. We can walk in armed with our feelings as our only response, or we can be ready to fight, holding God's Word firmly in our hearts and speaking it over ourselves and our people.

Last, I like to think of prayer as the water we get to drink while running. You can run without drinking water, but it's not nearly as enjoyable, and you won't finish as healthy as you could. Take big gulps of the presence of God that's accessible to you, reminding you He is near. Take the refreshment that's offered to you by the power of the Holy Spirit.

If you're going to run on mission, you gotta dress the part. After all, no one wants to run naked.

GO SLOW ENOUGH TO BE SHIFTED

For most of my adult life, I've felt like the young one. I've always felt like I was a freshman sitting at the juniors' table, hoping no one would notice that I don't even have my learner's permit yet. I got married at twenty, had my first baby at twenty-two, my second baby at twenty-three, and my third baby at twenty-four. By the time I was twenty-five, I was a mom of three and in full-time ministry. By the time I was thirty-one, my husband and I had planted a church, we'd moved about a dozen times, had four kids, I'd published a book and was writing another, and I was traveling a good bit to speak to women about the Lord.

These are all beautiful, God-given things, and I don't take these gifts or opportunities lightly. But in all honesty, my biggest fear is that everyone will see I'm as inexperienced and out-of-place as I feel. In my heart I feel this huge apprehension to express my fears and insecurities to others, because I'm always sure they'll just say, "Well—you're too young for all this anyhow. Go back to the sandbox where you belong."

I've found solace in 1 Timothy 4:12, which encourages us not to allow anyone to look down on us because we're young, but instead to set an example for others in speech, conduct, love, faith, and purity. I've tried to believe the truth that God decides when someone is ready for ministry and assuaged my heart with the factoid that Mary, the mother of Jesus, was probably only in her early teens when she got pregnant with Him. If Mary can handle being the mother of the Savior of the world as a teenager, surely God can prepare me for whatever ministry He has, even in my late twenties and early thirties.

But here's the deal—there's so much more to that 1 Timothy passage, and I think it has some wisdom for those of us who are running. Here's a little bit more from that passage in *The Message* translation:

> And don't let anyone put you down because you're young. Teach believers with your life: by word, by demeanor, by love, by faith, by integrity. Stay at your post reading Scripture, giving counsel, teaching. And that special gift of ministry you were given when the leaders of the church laid hands on you and prayed—keep that dusted off and in use. Cultivate these things. Immerse yourself in them. The people will all see you mature right before their eyes! Keep a firm grasp on

both your character and your teaching. Don't be diverted. Just keep at it. Both you and those who hear you will experience salvation. (1 Timothy 4:12–16 MSG)

It takes some serious grace and maturity to run on mission, fast and strong, no matter your age—without getting dragged down by naysayers who tell you that you're going too fast, too early, too hard, or the wrong way. I asked a few friends today what some of their biggest struggles with mission and calling are, and they almost all replied with some answer about people speaking discouragement over what they felt God asking them to do. It doesn't matter if you're thirty or thirteen—when you feel a passion for being used by God, it seems the first thing you'll experience as you step into that calling is some opposition from humans. Your dad might tell you that you don't know what you're getting into, your friends might laugh at your unbridled passion for ministry, your pastor may fear you're taking it too far, your husband might worry that you don't have enough time, and your family may be the first people who tell you you're not equipped for whatever it is you've set your eyes on.

I've found that bold humility seems to be the only answer for moving forward in these situations. When you fight and yell and act defensively, you prove that you might not be qualified to handle difficult things. When you shrink back and give up easily, you do the exact same thing, just from a different angle. It takes some humble confidence in Christ and His leading to allow people to ask you hard questions, sit in the tension when you don't have the answers, and invite the maturing process that will inevitably come.

It's easier to make a plan that says, "Here's this thing I'm called to do! I know it will be hard! I know I'm up against a fight! Here's why I know I can do it and do it better than anyone else has in the past." It's much harder, much more nuanced, and way wiser to say something like this instead: "I feel like God has called me to this. I don't know as much about it as I could, and I'm totally willing to learn more. I'd love for you to ask me hard questions, and I'll ask for your grace if I don't know the answers yet. I want to learn from people who've gone before me, and I want to do this ministry in a way that sets me up for success and gives God the most glory."

To run far, we've got to run slow enough to be shifted and to grow in the process. There's a reason why fast runs are called sprints. They're fast, but they're short. When you run a sprint, your head is down, your gaze is set—there is no time to talk or get refreshment or stop and tie your shoe if you fall. But the mission of God in our lives is like an ultra-ultra-ultra marathon. If we're lucky, we're in for years and years of missions, decades of ministry that give God glory. So we've got to slow down enough to be shifted as we go. It will take humility, grace, and sometimes the discernment to know when to listen, who to listen to, and when to keep going without more advice. The good news is, this is the exact discernment God promises us in the power of the Holy Spirit: our running partner, coach, and all-around good helper.

FEET BEFORE HANDS BEFORE MOUTH

I first heard the phrase, "Earn the right to be heard" in college when I was delving into different types of ministries and learning to share the gospel with people. The idea behind the phrase is that if we become fixtures in people's lives, showing up consistently and allowing them to see we'll be present for them, we'll eventually gain an invitation to share the gospel with them. While I think there are exceptions to this rule for sure, and occasionally there are extreme ministry circumstances that call for speaking truth no matter the amount of relational equity we've put in, this slogan has slowly become a massive fixture in my life on mission and I'm grateful to be reminded of the wisdom in it.

I'm a prophet through and through, and I like to speak into the problems I see in this world. It's not that I'm overly negative or nit-picky; it's just that the bend of my heart, the way it's created, is to call out issues and fix them wherever I can. In my first ministry job on staff at a church in college, I learned how you can quickly ruin a relationship when you use your mouth, or even your hands, without first using your feet.

I'll never forget being called into my overseeing pastor's office, or the way he gingerly played with his pen as he delivered the gentle correction that would shape the rest of my life. I laugh about it now, but I'm sure I cried big old tears that day—out of shame and regret, and the fear that I'd never figure out ministry. He told me there was a whole huge toolbox of ministry tools at our disposal, but that I seemed to use only the hammer, and in my wake I was leaving a lot of bruised high school girls who couldn't quite figure out why their new youth group leader kept yelling at them. In my mind I wasn't yelling, I was just pointing out the problems I saw (IMMODEST CLOTHING! OBSESSION WITH BOYS! TOO EXPENSIVE PURSES!), but I was failing to acknowledge that so much of ministry happens with the feet.

We've got to *walk with* people. We've got to *go to* people.

We've got to *stand firm* on our own holy ground while engaging in relationship with them. The alternatives are sitting passively by while life happens or running in the opposite direction because the people we're called to are in sin. Neither of these are good solutions. If our feet don't carry us to where they are, we'll never get to use our hands to serve them or our mouths to speak truth to them.

When we're on mission outside of our country or even outside of our context, let's say in short-term ministry, it's totally appropriate to also use our hands. What I mean is that when we build houses or provide medical aid, when we take blankets to the homeless shelter, when we feed the hungry or clothe the naked—our feet are taking us to them and our hands are doing the work, and this is a beautiful combination that I'm not knocking in the slightest. Maybe our mouth is even getting involved if we're speaking life and pointing to Jesus, but we're not there to rebuke or correct the hurting—we're just being the hands and the feet of our Savior to the ones who need Him most.

But for long-term ministry, the business of making disciples, the mouth eventually has to come into play using a more diverse array of tools. We've got to bring encouragement, and occasionally, correction. Our people may need admonishment, prayer, exhortation, and teaching. But before our mouths come into play, they're going to see what our hands can do, and before the hands get to work, our feet have to actually take us there.

There is ministry right where you're at, sweet friend, but you may have to stand up and walk over to it to participate. Earn the right to be heard; let your feet and your presence alert the world that you're there and ready for action.

THE MESS IS IN THE MINISTRY

As I was coming to the close of this book, and this chapter specifically, I asked my sweet mom for any wisdom she might want to share. We can all probably think of people who are famous on earth for their mission, but it's the people who are famous to us for the way they've been on mission in our own lives that leave the most impact, right? When I asked my sweet mama what she hopes women know about mission, she replied with a truth that made me giggle and feel relief all at once. She said, "I want all women to know that ministry is messy. It doesn't all look like a Samaritan's Purse advertisement. It's okay, in fact it's even better, when it looks like real-life women doing real ministry, even when they mess it up."

I believe there is an immense amount of abundance for us here, women. This life of dancing in grace and standing in our holiness and running on mission is God's best plan for us. I think it's thrilling, redeeming, fun, rewarding, and full of adventure, excitement, purpose, and blessing. But God help us if we think for some reason it's not going to be messy too.

We are going to keep sinning and needing Jesus, just because we will always feel the effects of this fallen world. We're going to get sick and tired and need to take breaks to care for our soul and turn our eyes back to Jesus. There will be seasons where we get corrected and have to sit out of the race for a minute. We're going to make messes, and we're going to do things wrong. We're going to have to ask for forgiveness, and unfortunately, we're going to turn people away from Jesus—even when that's the absolute last thing we want to do. We'll say stupid stuff and offend people, we'll let pride get the best of us, we'll lose our focus on what matters, and we'll have to clean up our messes or at least watch gratefully as Jesus does the damage control.

We are not the saviors; He is. We are not the answer; we just know the One who is. We are not the solution; we're still kind of part of the problem. And we can lose heart here or we can be bolstered by the good news that this is what our Father is in the business of: using messy people to bring other messy people to the light.

There's going to be a victorious finish to this long race, but it's best that right now we decide who will be getting the praise in that glory moment. True story: If we don't think too hard about it, we can assume it's us. We can picture ourselves crossing the finish line and pumping through the beautiful red ribbon having run hard and spent our lives devoted to the work and ministry of Jesus. We can picture the saints cheering us on, chanting our names, and the Father embracing us with the "good and faithful servant" deal. But in that scenario, we've left out two incredibly important facts: (1) It was His strength and His power that did all the heavy lifting along the way, and (2) It was His glory to be grabbed at the finish.

Jesus is the author and perfecter of our faith, not the coach who guides us through our own triumphant arrival to heaven. And in His name, I pray this helps you take the biggest, deepest, sigh of relief, because *this race is not about you.* It's not your name on the line. It's for Him and His glory *and* your joy and abundance, but it's His workmanship and His redemption and His plan and His blood making a way for us. This is the good news; this is our mission; this is our invitation to run. He's already won this race! And by faith, because of Jesus, we get to take part in the victory.

Let's Study the Word:

HEBREWS 10:23–25

Let us hold unswervingly to the hope we profess, for he who promised is faithful. And let us consider how we may spur one another on toward love and good deeds, not giving up meeting together, as some are in the habit of doing, but encouraging one another—and all the more as you see the Day approaching.

Who has God called you to run alongside? If you can't immediately start making a list, pray now and ask Him to open your eyes to see other believers He's put in your path so you can encourage each other on mission.

If still no one comes to mind, I want to encourage you: *Do not lose hope.* You can position yourself in a body of believers who are full of hope and running after the Lord by finding a local church. Go find the pastor or any leader after the Sunday service and say: "I want to be on mission. I want to be a disciple maker. But I need encouragement and people to run with me!" I promise you, they'll be thrilled.

In some cases we've got to gather and lead people to mission in order to have people to run with. If you're a leader who is already trying to point your people toward mission and you feel lonely, I hear you. That struggle is real. But keep going; keep pressing on. You'll be shifted, and your mission will be refined as you lead other people to make disciples while you make disciples. He is the prize, so keep going!

Let's Take It a Little Further

1. Reread Ephesians 6. Which piece of clothing are you forgetting to put on before running on mission? What would life look like if you got fully dressed?
2. Have you believed the lie that ministry was supposed to be tidy and lost hope when it got messy and real? Spend a few minutes praying. Ask God to help you let go of what you'd pictured and embrace what He has planned for your big, beautiful run.

Chapter 10

LET'S GO

STEPPING INTO THE CHOREOGRAPHY OF THE ABUNDANT LIFE

Read by Brittany Corner

I was walking into Vacation Bible School, a sweaty and slightly tired work-from-home mom, glad I'd planned a diversion for my kids during the first week of summer. I'd dropped off all four of them that morning and gotten a few hours of work in, and I was preparing my heart to dive in deep with them in the afternoon, playing and relaxing and transitioning into rest after a long school year. But as I walked to their classrooms, something felt different. I'm a sensitive old gal, and something was amiss or out of place. I just couldn't put my finger on it.

I was navigating the halls of this foreign-to-me-megachurch (our tiny downtown church can't quite yet pull off its own VBS), and I realized all the rooms were quiet. There were no errant children stabbing each other with fake swords, and I couldn't hear any mass games being played. A few peeks in the windows of the classrooms as I passed showed me that they were doing some serious Bible discussion with these kids and I was suddenly filled with anticipation to see how the kids had responded.

My kids are pastor's kids through and through; they meet all the stereotypes, and I love them for it. One minute they'll be talking about the new heaven and the new earth, and in the next minute they'll be getting thrown out of children's ministry for biting each other. They have heard us talk about Jesus nearly every day since they were born, and they've been presented with the option to believe in Him and have a relationship with Him since they could comprehend what that meant. I've always been grateful that they received my "no filter" gene, because they've always been honest with us regarding salvation.

My oldest son came to know Jesus the day before his fifth birthday, when he found us crying as we were packing to move. The Lord had miraculously broken his heart, he felt the weight of his sin, and he wanted to feel the peace of Christ in there instead. If you're *oohing* and *ahhhing* over that, you should know it hasn't gone this way with the other kids. Since Elias gave his heart to Jesus, we'll occasionally throw out the notion that the others might want to believe in Him and profess their love for Him too—but they always just tell us, "Nope, we're good."

They often say, "Maybe one day I'll give my heart to Jesus, but not today." Or if someone at church casually asks if they have a relationship with God, they might reply, "Not yet! Elias does, but not me." I have to tell you, I'm so grateful for their candor when it comes to this situation. I hope they always feel the eternal weight of a relationship with God and the freedom to be vulnerable that comes from being genuine about where you are with Him. We're also able to pray for them much more fervently when they're clear about where their hearts are.

So back to this summer day, as I was walking the halls, I was thinking, *Wouldn't it be funny if one of my kids gave their heart to Jesus, here at VBS, when we've presented them with the gospel so many times? Lord—let it be.* I went to Glory's class first, and you could have knocked me over with a feather when she burst out of the room before all the other kids, declaring, "MOM! YOU'LL NEVER GUESS WHAT I JUST DID!"

I pray I never forget how the rest of that day unfolded. Glory went on to tell me about how the VBS workers presented the salvation plan, how it was the same thing she'd heard from us over and over, but how something in her heart was "all mixed up" this time. She told me her hands shook as they asked her if she wanted to pray to receive Jesus. She told me she said no the first time, then felt like she was going to vomit, so she went back to the front of the room and said yes.

I got the kids in the car as our sweet girl talked a mile a minute telling us what had just transpired. I took all four of them to the grocery store to grab some food for lunch, and in the twenty minutes we were there, Glory found two grown women to witness to. She told them how she'd just started her relationship with God and boldly insinuated they needed to do the same. When we got back in the car, we called Nick on FaceTime, and she replayed the whole story for him, telling him with not a little audacity that she wanted to be baptized TODAY, at the beach, by him. He had misty eyes as he told her yes, of course, he'd meet us there. We texted all our family and asked if they could join us at the ocean in a few hours. Elias decided he wanted in on the baptism action. He hadn't been baptized, even though he'd given his life to the Lord four years prior. The rest is all sweet, beautiful memories.

Glory was her normal, sassy self during the baptism and the

celebration dinner afterward, and she laughed like a maniac when I tucked her into bed that night and reminded her, "Now we're not just mother and daughter; we're sisters." She was still Glory, but Glory with a new heart, Glory with a new worldview, Glory with an eternal life in Christ.

In the midst of that sweet summer day, I stole away for a few minutes to text my friend Rachael and tell her the amazing news. She wrote back with all kinds of praise hands and crying emojis and the following words:

> THIS IS IT. This is ministry. This is mission. You've been over there working out your own salvation for your daughter to see, receiving the grace God gives you as she watches, speaking truth day in and day out, failing and messing up and trying again, and she comes to know Jesus. This is why we do what we do. All these little, everyday acts of faithfulness add up, don't they? This is it. This is mission.

I love doing ministry, love attending women's conferences and learning how to better serve in the church and in the world. I love being on mission. But that day, on the beach with my wild little daughter, knowing she'd just chosen to follow the same God I'm following, even after seeing all of my massive mistakes and misgivings, I got to experience the absolute best part of mission. I got to see this cycle of dancing, standing, and running to tell the good news come full circle with another new sister soul dancing in the glorious grace and new life only Christ can bring.

Days like that one remind me, this wasn't *our* grand idea. We didn't make up ministry because we wanted to make the world a better place or because we're just super humanitarians. We're the people of God, rescued from ourselves and the darkness of a purposeless life on earth and a dark and grave one in eternity. We're compelled by the love of a good God who pursues us from the get-go and never stops, always bringing us back into His peace and presence, always making a way for us to be in communion with Him. We're made holy by the blood of our Savior Jesus, placed on a firm foundation and rooted in an identity that can't be messed with. We're purchased with the love of a Father that can't be thwarted by any work on heaven, on earth, or by any powers of darkness or hell. We've been given new desires and convictions, new eyes to see the world around us, new ears to hear truth, and new appetites to hunger and thirst for righteousness.

All that has been done for us, to us, because it pleases Him and makes Him happy, but what's more, He has invited us into this work—not because He needs us, but because being an ambassador in this kingdom is the equivalent of abundance, or indescribable fullness, in our lives.

We are the daughters of God, and we get to dance, stand, and run for the glory of God and the joy of our own lives. It might not have been our idea in the first place, but sure enough, it is our reality. And that's some good news.

THERE'S MORE AT STAKE HERE

"Here's another way to put it: You're here to be light, bringing out the God-colors in the world. God is not a secret to be kept. We're going public with this, as public as a city on a hill. If I make you light-bearers, you don't think I'm going to hide you under a bucket, do you? I'm putting you on a light stand. Now that I've put you there on a hilltop, on a light stand—shine! Keep an open house, be generous with your lives. By opening up to others, you'll prompt people to open up with God, this generous Father in heaven." (Matthew 5:14–16 MSG)

The days of a binary faith are over. We don't live in a black-and-white world that only believes in a hell-prevention salvation. You see the beautiful cycle of grace, holiness, and mission—don't you? Our biographies of faith are these messy, woven tapestries of overlapping stories. They're ripe with sanctification and redemption and forgiveness and the gospel—we don't have flat timelines that only recognize lost and then found. God's story in our lives is far more dynamic than that.

There is more at stake here than just salvation, which is why this isn't a book written to convince you to place your eternal life in His hands. I'm in the camp that believes the whole idea of believing in Jesus is actually a pretty easy pitch. First, I think the Holy Spirit does all the work and breaks our hearts at the appropriate time so that we have eyes to see we need a Savior. Second, I believe that even on paper—even logistically—life with Christ is a good bet to make. All you have to do is believe and confess that you think He's the way to heaven; you don't have to physically do anything. Let's say you try that and nothing happens—you never experience Him or sense that you've made a right choice. You can't get any money back because you didn't give any to get Him, but I guess you could ask for your eternal placeholder to be moved to the hell bracket? Well, actually—you can't do that. He accounts for our lack of faith and seals up our hearts and says that nothing can snatch His love and identity out of our souls once we've confessed and He's placed His promise there.

But here's what we know, women of God. Just like no one ever says they regret a workout after it's over, no one ever says they regret the intimacy they experienced with the one true God of the universe. People might say they regret what they were exposed to in the context of religion, they might regret something they did or said as a result of an interpretation of Scripture, or they might even regret joining a certain body of believers. But when it comes to Jesus and the Father and the Holy Spirit, I've never met someone who's had an encounter with the triune Godhead and thought, "Eh. I could take it or leave it."

And that's because we serve a God who isn't just into moving names from the naughty to the nice list; we serve a God who sent His Son to die a painful and excruciating death, becoming the embodiment of shame and damnation, so we can have abundant life this side of heaven—not just eternal life in a world to come. His plan is so bold and big it encompasses both! Our God is not a stifling God; His kingdom doesn't look gray and colorless. He's into painting our everyday lives with colors much more creative and brilliant.

Friends, sisters—my concern for us isn't fearful, it isn't stern, and my arms aren't crossed in disappointment. But my heart feels the ache that we are truly lacking the lavish joy, excitement, purpose, healing, hope, and pleasure of living grace-saturated lives of mission while rooted in the holy identity we've been given by God our Father. I'm not worried that we're going to mess it up; I'm worried that if we don't begin making the God-inspired moves of women set apart, we're going to miss out on what could have been.

As beautiful as that day with Glory on the beach was, I know it wasn't the brightest or most intimate day she'll ever have in her life as a believer. Her journey didn't end at salvation; it began. And I for one pray, hope, and trust that her most abundant and vibrant days are ahead of her. Sister, I pray, hope, and trust the same can be said for you and me as we step into the grace-filled lives of mission, standing firm on the holy ground God has given us.

LET'S GO

Because we all do better with a little positive reinforcement, will you indulge me while I paint a picture of a season that I think we could step into? A season we would craft with our relationships and lives? Will you let me describe what I think it could look like to dance, stand, and run?

I know you all are the choir—you're the faithful, you're the ones whose hearts are already tuned to hear His voice and see His hand. I know you're the choir, and I bless and encourage your humility in reading a book that is so seemingly about the basics: grace, holiness, and mission. But I've heard it said that you preach to the choir for one reason alone, and that's to get them to sing. This is a time when the women of God deeply need to hear one another's voices, rising louder in victorious harmony in praise of a good God. They need a song that is louder than the fighting, the should-ing and shaming, the striving and slander. We need a new song of truth, and I'm begging you, choir, come sing with me.

Come sing and step into the choreography of the abundant life.

Your Invitation to Dance

I can picture us, the women of God, stepping into a new season of understanding grace. In this scene, women are learning to love the grace they're being consistently and lavishly given from the Father. Of course they feel the weight of their daily sin and brokenness, but they find their identities rooted in sainthood more than they find it in their sin. And as it turns out, they sin LESS where grace abounds! When they recognize the areas wherein they fall short, and then dance in the mercy and forgiveness they've been given, they're so much less prone to keep on sinning. Their eyes aren't closed by defiance, and their hearts aren't made heavy with pride. Not only do they dance in the grace they've been given, but they want it for everyone around them.

Since they're quick to repent, they're also quick to forgive—they know they can continually expect to need Jesus themselves and they also anticipate the people they're in community with needing Him as well. Neediness is no longer a bad word among these women of God; they don't apologize for their tears or their prayers or their tenderness. They're not afraid of grace; they dance to the rhythm of freedom since they're no longer chained to obligation or condemnation; they've got the margin to tether their hearts to the love of their actual lives, Jesus. They want to go where He goes and follow where He's leading, and they don't just know they've been rescued; they know where it is He has rescued them to.

Your Invitation to Stand

These women of God, these daughters of the King know where they came from (death, despair, brokenness, darkness, sin, condemnation, and shame), but more importantly—yes MORE importantly—they know where He has brought them in His love and salvation. When they glance down, they find holy ground under their feet. It's not that they've worked to get here; it's not that they've earned their spot or stacked their accomplishments up to build a ladder up to God. They've been plucked and placed and covered in the blood of Jesus: Here stand the daughters of God, they're free and they're holy, and because He's said so, no one can say otherwise.

These women believe what God has said about them and *that* dictates the way they live. They have cast off the lie that the way they behave determines their identity. They are holy and they live as such—they speak life, they allow themselves to examine their motives, they believe that all that they own is God's anyhow, and they give it back to Him. They are set apart so they don't spend their days longing to belong, aching to be accepted, or striving to be included here on earth. They know their citizenship is in heaven and their home is there, so they see the world and all its inhabitants with kingdom eyes—everything on the path to eternity, every person redeemable, and every situation under the dominion of God.

These women sense their destiny and their place in this whole path to restitution; they know their gifts, desires, blessings, heartaches, and all of their stories are tools in the hands of a loving God trying to call His kids back home. They're not confusing who all of this is for, so they can look down at what they've been given and offer it back up to Him—for His story and His glory.

These women don't hang their head in condemnation, but they allow the Holy Spirit to do the work of shifting and correcting them. They ask themselves questions like, "Why am I doing *this*?" repeatedly, not because they're not at ease with who they are, but because they believe true refreshment comes after repentance. They're growing and they're changing and they're looking more like Jesus, all while knowing they still need Him. Never outgrowing their need for the gospel, the daughters of God stand firm in this place where He's put them, declaring that He has drawn pleasant boundary lines for them, and indeed, they have a glorious inheritance.

I can see a generation of women rising up who see more than two options for interacting with the world: rejecting it or conforming to it. They're not here to judge; they're here to speak life and share the light they've found in Christ alone. They can be inside the world, living and moving and interacting, building relationships and lives with people who might not believe the same things they do. But they're very much set apart in that they have a different home and different identities and a different purpose. These women of God are not here to build kingdoms, lasting memories, honorable reputations, hot bodies, cute wardrobes, or names for themselves. These women are here to be loved by God and to tell other people what a joy it is to be loved by Him.

Your Invitation to Run

The daughters of God who have such a firm and delighted grasp on the grace that has marked them, these women who know where they stand on holy and sacred ground, when you ask them what they're doing, they'll answer with mission. It's not that God needs them to get stuff done, but it's their absolute joy to have been invited into His kingdom ministry and they are running with all they've got. If you ask them to be truly honest about their purpose here on earth, they'll tell you with resolution that they want as many people to know what they know: life doesn't have to end at the grave and it doesn't have to be lackluster when we're here on earth either. Christ died that we might have eternal peace and hope and LIFE after we die, but He also died that we might have access to the heavenly riches of His peace, strength, purpose, and authority while we're still on this side of eternity.

These women are using their hands, their feet, their voices, to push back the kingdom of darkness and usher in the reign of life. It doesn't mean that they're preaching all the time and it doesn't mean they're running themselves ragged, but they are counting the call they've been given as ambassadors an honor—they're grateful to have a place at the table and a role in the work.

And the cycle goes round and round. From darkness to dancing in grace. From lost to being found on holy ground. From spinning and striving and sitting on our hands, to getting up on our feet and running on mission, with the revolution beginning again and again, each time a daughter gets baptized or a friend professes her faith. Every time a new sister's name is written in the Book of Life, because these disciple-makers, these holy women of God, took Him at His Word and believed when He said that this is what they were made to do.

This is it.

This is why we do it.

This is our mission.

This is our life abundant.

We dance, stand, and run for the glory of God.

You in?

A *DANCE, STAND, RUN* GLOSSARY

Here's the deal, friends. We're going to go to some heavy places in this book, so I want us all to be on some solid ground before we do. We're going to throw around words like *holy*, *grace*, *righteousness*, and *sin*, and if I may, I'd love to offer a working definition of those meatier words. A Gal's Guide to Big Words, if you will. These definitions are adapted mainly from the *Baker Compact Dictionary of Theological Terms*, but they're heavily supplemented by input from my girlfriends and my own weirdo vernacular. Enjoy.

Abundance: (Greek: perissos) Abundance essentially means *more*. Exceedingly more, going past the expected limit. In our children's ministry, we describe abundance as an overflowing cup. There's more than you expect and more than you can perceive (if you're the cup). I don't know about you, but children's ministry illustrations always help me a lot. Example in the Bible: John 10:10, "The thief comes only to steal and kill and destroy; I have come that they may have life, and have it to the full."

Consecrate: (Hebrew: qadash) To consecrate is to set apart. God sets apart holy things for His glory and their good. He set the Sabbath apart from the rest of the week; He set His children apart from the rest of the world. He often set particular people apart from those they'd be leading so they'd be distinguished. We (believers) are consecrated in love, by grace, to be a people of His possession to call others into marvelous light. Example in the Bible: Exodus 19:10, "And the Lord said to Moses, 'Go to the people and consecrate them today and tomorrow.'"

Gospel: (Greek: euaggelion) Gospel is literally just a Greek word that means good news. The good news of Christ for us is simply this: Jesus, the Son of God, came and lived a sinless human life, died to pay the price for the sins of humankind, was buried, and rose again. When we hear this and believe it, we can receive grace through faith and be made new by the Spirit of God, united with Christ, and adopted into God's family. Example in the Bible: Acts 20:24, "However, I consider my life worth nothing to me; my only aim is to finish the race and complete the task the Lord Jesus has given me—the task of testifying to the good news of God's grace."

Grace: (Greek: charis) Grace is the part of God's character that describes the gifts He gives us that we don't deserve. When we get mercy, patience, love, favor, and faithfulness, this is grace, as we not only didn't earn it, but our bad behavior should prevent us from getting it. When you break down the Greek word, you get a picture of God leaning toward us, giving Himself away. So let's put it all together: Grace is God leaning toward us, giving us all the good stuff we don't deserve, because He loves us. Example in the Bible: Romans 3:23–24, "For all have sinned and fall short of the glory of God, and all are justified freely by his grace through the redemption that came by Christ Jesus."

Holiness (God's): (Hebrew: qadosh) Holiness is God's set-apartness, His exaltedness above all created things, including us. His holiness encompasses the truth that He is pure, not corrupted by sin, and able to call other things holy (see consecration, above). In short, God is absolutely and infinitely better than everything else—He's the definition of good, great, amazing, incredible, and right. He's holy. Example in the Bible: Psalm 111:9, "He provided redemption for his people; he ordained his covenant forever—holy and awesome is his name."

Holiness (humanity's): (Greek: hagiazó) This word refers to an object that is called holy because God says so. It means that something has been purified, set apart, and should be treated as sacred. This is a description of our holiness. While we don't earn this, God makes it so when He pays for our souls with the blood of Jesus (see imputation, below). Because God has called us holy and set apart, we cannot become more holy or less holy. We can act in a way that acknowledges our holy standing, but we can't do anything to lose it or improve it. This is so important. If we are in Christ, we are holy. Example in the Bible: Hebrews 10:10, "And by that will, we have been made holy through the sacrifice of the body of Jesus Christ once for all."

Imputation: (Greek: ellogeó) Imputation is a spiritual act of imparting. It's one of the ways God takes His love too far in the best ways. He doesn't just save us and let us enjoy His own righteousness, He takes His righteousness and makes it ours. He has to remain just while also being loving. To be just and holy, to fulfill His own law, the only way for us to be in relationship with His righteousness is to receive His righteousness. Imputation is also synonymous with "crediting." God credits us His good stuff and calls it ours. Example in the Bible: Romans 5:13, "To be sure, sin was in the world before the law was given, but sin is not charged against anyone's account where there is no law."

Mission: Mission, as a word, isn't necessarily found in the Bible, but it's a concept we see in Matthew 28 at Jesus's Great Commission to His disciples. He charges them to make disciples of all nations. When we speak about personal missions or corporate missions, it's important to keep this objective in mind. Other versions of this word we might hear and use frequently: missional (to be of the mind-set that what you're doing is intended to make disciples) and mission-minded (this would describe people who are thinking about making disciples or keeping this at the forefront of what they're doing).

Righteousness (God's): (Hebrew: tsedeq) This is a characteristic of God that is pretty simple. It basically means that God is always right. He cannot not be right, or He would cease to be God. He must always be accurate and just. He must act according to standards that reflect His holy nature. Example in the Bible: Psalm 9:4, "For you have upheld my right and my cause, sitting enthroned as the righteous judge."

Sin: (Greek: hamartia) Sin literally means to miss the mark. We sin in our hearts and in our deeds (or lack thereof), in any way we live that doesn't line up with God's code of perfection. Therefore sin is what separates us from being in perfect communion with God since His holiness makes Him exalted above all things imperfect. Example in the Bible: Matthew 1:21, "She will give birth to a son, and you are to give him the name Jesus, because he will save his people from their sins."

THANK YOU

I'm thankful for you, Jesus. My best friend and the fighter who won my soul. I'm thankful for the Holy Spirit that continually pokes at me and comforts me, makes me sick over my own sin and overwhelmed by a God I can't see. I'm thankful for you, Father, for always pursuing and never just "allowing" me. This book is for you, Lord. You did the heavy lifting and should get all the glory.

Nick has told me for years: you can write a book or run a marathon; you can't do both at once. When he first started saying that phrase, it wasn't literal. I didn't have plans to write a book OR run a marathon, he was just trying to teach me about wisdom and setting realistic boundaries. The only problem is, I never did learn how to set those boundaries and in this particular season I *did* attempt to write a book *and* run a marathon, all at once. Literally and figuratively.

And in the middle of the literal marathon and the literal book writing process, there were multiple occasions where I'd break down, crying out in my weakness, sure that I couldn't go on. And wouldn't you know? My people never said, "I told you so . . ." and never shook their heads at me for biting off more than I could chew. They only ever spoke of God's strength and reminded me of His goodness.

Nick, thank you for helping me live more wisely every day, while also encouraging me to be the wild woman God made me. Thank you for your incredibly humble, upside down, kingdom-minded leadership. Thank you for your kindness that helps me live a life of repentance a lot easier. Thanks for cooking dinner most nights and for being so stinking handsome.

To the people who've carried me through this marathon season: Katie, Mom, Rach, Caroline, Kristen, Krista, and Sarah, thank you for running with me figuratively and literally. Thank you for being the best people a girl could ever ask for. I hope I love you half as well as you love me.

I'm crazy thankful for the women of Gospel Community who have taken a bet on building a family that dances in grace as we learn to also stand in our holiness. Let's run together for a very long time. Let's rally.

Thank you to the All Good Things gals for walking this new fresh season with me. Helen, Melissa, and Hannah: I'm excited for the stories we'll tell and grateful for the lives we get to impact together.

To my prayer/reading team, who were essentially the midwives of this book. Morgan, Kelly, Gina, Jensine, Ann, Mere, Hannah, and Britt: THANK YOU! THANK YOU! You didn't have to do that and I know this book wouldn't have been what it needed to be without you. I wouldn't be who I'm supposed to be without you. Hannah and Britt, you gals specifically, I'll never forget riding in the back of the car reading you the first chapter, scared out of my mind. Thank you for telling me to keep going.

Lauren Pavao, I don't deserve a friend as wise and generous as you. Thank you for giving what only you could and doing it so graciously.

Elias, Glo, Benja, and Cannon, I know you didn't pick to have a mom who writes books and picks you up from school looking like a zombie, but I'm grateful you love me all the same. You guys are my best friends and my favorite story to tell always.

The Dance, Stand, Run Facebook group! You brave, free women! You've helped shaped this book so much and you're shaping our generation in a beautiful way by being such great leaders. You're redeeming Facebook in a big way and making it great again.

Last, but most definitely not least: Jenni Burke, thank you for not thinking your author was nuts when I sent you a wide-eyed, wild email asking to change the whole book. Thanks for caring more about what God wants than anything else. Alicia Kasen, I put you through the wringer on this one and no amount of flowers will ever make up for it! Thank you for still loving me and helping me push. Stephanie Smith, thank you for taking a kooky manifesto and turning it into something He can use to grab the hearts of His girls and speak life over them.